Cyber Safety

EC-Council | Press

This title maps to

Security | 5™

COURSE TECHNOLOGY
CENGAGE Learning™

Australia • Brazil • Japan • Korea • Mexico • Singapore • Spain • United Kingdom • United States

COURSE TECHNOLOGY
CENGAGE Learning™

Cyber Safety: EC-Council | Press

Course Technology/Cengage Learning
Staff:

Vice President, Career and Professional
Editorial: Dave Garza

Director of Learning Solutions:
Matthew Kane

Executive Editor: Stephen Helba

Managing Editor: Marah Bellegarde

Editorial Assistant: Meghan Orvis

Vice President, Career and
Professional Marketing: Jennifer Baker

Marketing Director: Deborah Yarnell

Marketing Manager: Erin Coffin

Marketing Coordinator: Shanna Gibbs

Production Director: Carolyn Miller

Production Manager: Andrew Crouth

Content Project Manager:
Brooke Greenhouse

Senior Art Director: Jack Pendleton

EC-Council:

President | EC-Council: Sanjay Bavisi

Sr. Director US | EC-Council:
Steven Graham

For product information and technology assistance, contact us at
Cengage Learning Customer & Sales Support, 1-800-354-9706

For permission to use material from this text or product,
submit all requests online at **www.cengage.com/permissions**.
Further permissions questions can be e-mailed to
permissionrequest@cengage.com

Library of Congress Control Number: 2009932552

ISBN-13: 978-1-4354-8371-2

ISBN-10: 1-4354-8371-5

Cengage Learning
5 Maxwell Drive
Clifton Park, NY 12065-2919
USA

Cengage Learning is a leading provider of customized learning solutions with office locations around the globe, including Singapore, the United Kingdom, Australia, Mexico, Brazil, and Japan. Locate your local office at: **international.cengage.com/region**

Cengage Learning products are represented in Canada by
Nelson Education, Ltd.

For more learning solutions, please visit our corporate website at **www.cengage.com**

Printed in the United States of America
1 2 3 4 5 6 7 12 11 10 09

Brief Table of Contents

Table of Contents

Hacking and electronic crimes sophistication has grown at an exponential rate in recent years. In fact, recent reports have indicated that cyber crime already surpasses the illegal drug trade! Unethical hackers, better known as *black hats*, are preying on information systems of government, corporate, public, and private networks, constantly testing the security mechanisms of these organizations to the limit with the sole aim of exploiting them and profiting from the exercise. High-profile crimes have proven that the traditional approach to computer security is simply not sufficient, even with the strongest perimeter, properly configured defense mechanisms such as firewalls, intrusion detection, and prevention systems, strong end-to-end encryption standards, and anti-virus software. Hackers have proven their dedication and ability to systematically penetrate networks all over the world. In some cases, black hats can execute attacks so flawlessly that they can compromise a system, steal everything of value, and completely erase their tracks in less than 20 minutes.

The EC-Council | Press is dedicated to stopping hackers in their tracks.

About EC-Council

The International Council of Electronic Commerce Consultants, better known as EC-Council was founded in late 2001 to address the need for well-educated and certified information security and e-business practitioners. EC-Council is a global, member-based organization comprised of industry and subject matter experts all working together to set the standards and raise the bar in information security certification and education.

EC-Council first developed the *Certified Ethical Hacker,* C|EH program. The goal of this program is to teach the methodologies, tools, and techniques used by hackers. Leveraging the collective knowledge from hundreds of subject matter experts, the C|EH program has rapidly gained popularity around the globe and is now delivered in more than 70 countries by more than 450 authorized training centers with more than 60,000 information security practitioners trained. C|EH is the benchmark for many government entities and major corporations around the world. Shortly after C|EH was launched, EC-Council developed the *Certified Security Analyst,* E|CSA. The goal of the E|CSA program is to teach groundbreaking analysis methods that must be applied while conducting advanced penetration testing. E|CSA led to the *Licensed Penetration Tester,* L|PT status. The *Computer Hacking Forensic Investigator,* C|HFI was formed with the same design methodologies and has become a global standard in certification for computer forensics. EC-Council, through its impervious network of professionals and huge industry following, has developed various other programs in information security and e-business. EC-Council certifications are viewed as the essential certifications needed when standard configuration and security policy courses fall short. Providing a true, hands-on, tactical approach to security, individuals armed with the knowledge disseminated by EC-Council programs are securing networks around the world and beating the hackers at their own game.

About the EC-Council | Press

The EC-Council | Press was formed in late 2008 as a result of a cutting-edge partnership between global information security certification leader EC-Council and leading global academic publisher Cengage Learning. This partnership marks a revolution in academic textbooks and courses of study in information security, computer forensics, disaster recovery, and end-user security. By identifying the essential topics and content of EC-Council professional certification programs and repurposing this world class content to fit academic programs, the EC-Council | Press was formed. The academic community is now able to incorporate this powerful cutting edge content into new and existing information security programs. By closing the gap between academic study and professional certification, students and instructors are able to leverage the power of rigorous academic focus and high-demand industry certification. The EC-Council | Press is set to revolutionize global information security programs and ultimately create a new breed of practitioners capable of combating the growing epidemic of cybercrime and the rising threat of cyber-war.

Cyber Safety

The EC-Council | Press' newest product, *Cyber Safety*, is designed for anyone who is interested in learning computer networking and security basics. This book gives individuals the basic security literacy skills that prepare them for high-end IT academic or training programs. The book also prepares readers to take and succeed on the Security|5 certification exam from EC-Council.

Chapter Contents

Chapter 1, *Foundations of Security*, lays the groundwork for future topics by defining the terminology essential to understanding the concept of computer security. It also gives an overview of security, cyber crime, and the security process. Chapter 2, *Basic Security Procedures*, explains the basic security procedures or practices one can adopt to address security proactively. Chapter 3, *Desktop Security*, explores the challenges that arise in the workplace when securing computers. Chapter 4, *Administering Windows Securely*, introduces several of the built-in features of Microsoft Windows that can be used to work more securely. Chapter 5, *Security Threats and Attacks*, includes a discussion of the various security threats and attacks to which today's computer user is vulnerable. Chapter 6, *Incident Response*, conveys an understanding of what an incident response is and how to address it. Chapter 7, *Secure Internet Access*, discusses how to restrict site access, identify secure sites, and establish security for a wireless network access point. The last chapter, Chapter 8, *Working on the Internet*, discusses how to work safely on the Internet, including sending or transferring information and files; transacting business; communicating via instant messaging or file-sharing and dial-in networks; using portable, wireless, and USB devices; and using media files and third-party software.

Chapter Features

Many features are included in each chapter and all are designed to enhance the learner's learning experience. Features include:

- *Objectives* begin each chapter and focus the learner on the most important concepts in the chapter.
- *Key Terms* are designed to familiarize the learner with terms that will be used within the chapter.
- *Case Example*, found throughout the chapter, present short scenarios followed by questions that challenge learners to arrive at answers or solutions to the problems presented.
- *Chapter Summary*, at the end of each chapter, serves as a review of the key concepts covered in the chapter.
- *Review Questions* allow learners to test their comprehension of the chapter content.
- *Hands-On Projects* encourage learners to apply the knowledge they have gained after finishing the chapter.

Additional Resources

The Information Security Community Site was created for learners and instructors to find out about the latest in information security news and technology.
Visit *community.cengage.com/infosec* to:

- Learn what is new in information security through live news feeds, videos, and podcasts;
- Connect with peers and security experts through blogs and forums;
- Browse our online catalog.

Additional Instructor Resources

Free to all instructors who adopt the Cyber Safety product for their courses, a complete package of instructor resources is available. These resources are available from the Course Technology Web site, *www.cengage.com*, by going to the product page for this book in the online catalog, and choosing "Instructor Downloads." A username and password can be obtained from your Cengage Learning sales representative.

Resources include:

- *Instructor Manual*: This manual includes course objectives and additional information to help your instruction.
- *Examview Testbank*: This Windows-based testing software helps instructors design and administer tests and pre-tests. In addition to generating tests that can be printed and administered, this full-featured program has an online testing component that allows students to take tests at the computer and have their exams automatically graded.
- *PowerPoint Presentations*: This book comes with a set of Microsoft PowerPoint slides for each chapter. These slides are meant to be used as a teaching aid for classroom presentations, to be made available to students for chapter review, or to be printed for classroom distribution. Instructors are also at liberty to add their own slides.
- *Labs*: These are additional hands-on activities to provide additional practice for students.
- *Assessment Activities*: These additional assessment opportunities include discussion questions, writing assignments, Internet research activities, and homework assignments along with a final cumulative project.
- *Final Exam*: The exam provides a comprehensive assessment of Cyber Safety content.

How to Become Security|5 Certified

Security|5 certification utilizes the working knowledge a computer user possesses to achieve better efficiency in using computer resources securely. The certification is targeted toward today's knowledge workers who use computer resources in their daily activities. It tests them on practical aspects of security and networking which gives an advantage over common users who have not been educated with this respected base of content.

Security|5 Certification exams are available through Prometric Prime. To finalize your certification after your training, you must:

1. Purchase an exam voucher from the EC-Council Community site at Cengage Learning *(www.cengage.com/community/eccouncil)* if one was not purchased with your book.

2. **Speak with your instructor about scheduling an exam session, or visit the EC-Council Community site for more information.**

3. Take and pass the Security|5 certification examination with a score of 70 percent or better.

Other EC Council I Press Products

Network Security Administrator Series

The EC-Council I Press Network Administrator Series, E|NSA, is intended for those studying to become system administrators network administrators, or anyone interested in network security technologies. This series is designed to educate learners from a vendor neutral standpoint on how to defend the networks they manage. This series covers the fundamental skills in evaluating internal and external threats to network security and design, enforcing network level security policies, and ultimately protecting an organization's information. Covering a broad range of topics from secure network fundamentals, protocols and analysis, standards and policy, and hardening infrastructure, to configuring IPS, IDS and firewalls, bastion host and honeypots, learners completing this series will have full understanding of defensive measures taken to secure their organizations' information.

Books in Series
- *Network Defense: Fundamentals and Protocols/1435483553*
- *Network Defense: Security Policy and Threats/1435483561*
- *Network Defense: Perimeter Defense Mechanisms/143548357X*
- *Network Defense: Securing and Troubleshooting Network Operating Systems/1435483588*
- *Network Defense: Security and Vulnerability Assessment/1435483596*

Ethical Hacking and Countermeasures Series

The EC-Council | Press Ethical Hacking and Countermeasures Series is intended for those studying to become security officers, auditors, security professionals, site administrators, and anyone who is concerned about or responsible for the integrity of network infrastructure. The series includes a broad base of topics in offensive network security and ethical hacking, as well as network defense and countermeasures. The content of this program is designed to immerse tlearners into an interactive environment where they will be shown how to scan, test, hack, and secure information systems. A wide variety of tools, viruses, and malware is presented in this course, providing a complete understanding of the tactics and tools used by hackers. By gaining a thorough understanding of how hackers operate, ethical hackers are able to set up strong countermeasures and defensive systems to protect organizations' critical infrastructure and information.

Books in Series
- *Ethical Hacking and Countermeasures: Attack Phases*/143548360X
- *Ethical Hacking and Countermeasures: Threats and Defense Mechanisms*/1435483618
- *Ethical Hacking and Countermeasures: Web Applications and Data Servers*/1435483626
- *Ethical Hacking and Countermeasures: Linux, Macintosh and Mobile Systems*/1435483642
- *Ethical Hacking and Countermeasures: Secure Network Infrastructure*/1435483650

Security Analyst Series

The EC-Council | Press Security Analyst Series is intended for those studying to become network server administrators, firewall administrators, security testers, system administrators, or risk assessment professionals. This series covers a broad base of topics in advanced penetration testing and security analysis. The content of this program is designed to expose the learner to groundbreaking methodologies in conducting thorough security analysis, as well as advanced penetration testing techniques. Armed with the knowledge from the *Security Analyst* series, learners will be able to perform the intensive assessments required to effectively identify and mitigate risks to the security of organizations' infrastructures.

Books in Series
- *Certified Security Analyst: Security Analysis and Advanced Tools*/1435483669
- *Certified Security Analyst: Customer Agreements and Reporting Procedures in Security Analysis*/1435483677
- *Certified Security Analyst: Penetration Testing Methodologies in Security Analysis*/1435483685
- *Certified Security Analyst: Network and Communication Testing Procedures in Security Analysis*/1435483693
- *Certified Security Analyst: Network Threat Testing Procedures in Security Analysis*/1435483707

Computer Forensics Series

The EC-Council | Press Computer Forensics Series is intended for those studying to become police investigators or other law enforcement personnel, defense and military personnel, e-business security professionals, systems administrators, legal professionals, banking, insurance or other professionals, government agencies, or IT managers. The content of this program is designed to expose the learner to the process of detecting attacks and collecting evidence in a forensically sound manner with the intent to report crime and prevent future attacks. Advanced techniques in computer investigation and analysis with interest in generating potential legal evidence are included. In full, this series prepares learners to identify evidence in computer-related crime and abuse cases, as well as track intrusive hackers' paths through client systems.

Books in Series
- *Computer Forensics: Investigation Procedures and Response*/1435483499
- *Computer Forensics: Investigating Hard Disks, File and Operating Systems*/1435483502
- *Computer Forensics: Investigating Data and Image Files*/1435483510
- *Computer Forensics: Investigating Network Intrusions and Cybercrime*/1435483529
- *Computer Forensics: Investigating Wireless Networks and Devices*/1435483537

Wireless Safety/1435483766

Wireless|5 introduces the learner to the basics of wireless technologies and its practical adaptation. *Wireless|5* is tailored to cater to any individual's desire to learn more about wireless technology. It requires no pre-requisite knowledge and aims to educate the learner in simple applications of these technologies. Topics include wireless signal propagation, IEEE and ETSI Wireless Standards, WLANs and operation, wireless protocols and communication languages, wireless devices, and wireless security networks.

Network Safety /1435483774

Network|5 provides the basic core knowledge on how infrastructure enables a working environment. Intended for those in office environments and home users who wants to optimize resource utilization, share infrastructure, and make the best of technology and the convenience it offers. Topics include foundations of networks, networking components, wireless networks, basic hardware components, networking environments, and connectivity as well as troubleshooting.

Disaster Recovery Professional: Disaster Recovery /1435488709

Disaster Recovery Professional: Business Continuity/1435488695

The *Disaster Recovery Professional Series* introduces learners to the methods employed in identifying vulnerabilities and demonstrates how to take the appropriate countermeasures to prevent and mitigate failure risks for organizations. It also provides a foundation in disaster recovery principles, including preparation of a disaster recovery plan, assessment of risks in the enterprise, development of policies and procedures, and understanding of the roles and relationships of various members of organizations, implementation of the plan, and recovering from disasters. Students will learn how to create a secure network by putting policies and procedures in place and restoring a network in the event of a disaster.

Acknowledgement

The publisher would like acknowledge Jean McKay, who served as the subject matter expert reviewer for this book. Jean McKay is the president of PuttyCove, Inc., a firm specializing in project management training/consulting and IT technical instruction.

Jean holds numerous certifications issued by vendors in the IT industry including Microsoft, Cisco, Novell, EC-Council, and CompTIA, as well as the PMP, and PMP-RMP certifications sponsored by the Project Management Institute. A software developer, a manufacturing firm, and technical training companies formerly employed her as a senior trainer, LAN administrator, and project manager.

Planning and leading successful projects to completion, educating team members and other stakeholders in methods to improve their project management skills, and improving processes used on existing projects are among her work. With a focus on risk analysis, disaster recovery, and business continuity, she combines IT expertise with business objectives.

Foundations of Security

Objectives

After completing this chapter, you should be able to:

- Define essential terminology
- Define security
- Explain the need for security
- Understand what cyber crime is
- Recall information security statistics
- Discuss the ease-of-use triangle
- Recall security myths
- Know how to harden security

Key Terms

Assurance   confidence that the system will behave according to its specifications

Attack   an assault on system security that derives from an intelligent threat; an attack is any *action* that violates security

Authenticity   the identification and assurance of the origin of information

Availability   which is the ability to use the information or resource as desired

Confidentiality   which relates to preventing the disclosure of information to unauthorized persons

Cyber crime   any illegal act involving a computer, its systems, or its applications and the Internet

Exploit   a defined way to breach the security of an IT system through vulnerability

Exposure   security violation that results from a threat action

Integrity   the trustworthiness of data or resources in terms of preventing improper and unauthorized changes

Malware   a combination of the words *malicious* and *software*, it is any software designed to infiltrate or damage a computer without the user's knowledge or consent

Security a state of stability of information and infrastructure in which the possibility of successful yet undetected theft, tampering, and disruption of information and services is kept low or tolerable

Target of evaluation an IT system, product, or component that is identified as requiring security evaluation

Threat refers to a situation in which human or natural occurrences can cause an undesirable outcome

Trojan horse a program that seems to be useful or harmless but contains hidden code embedded to take advantage of or damage the computer on which it is run

Virus malicious code written with the intention to damage the victim's computer

Vulnerability existence of a weakness, design, or implementation error that can lead to an unexpected, undesirable event compromising the security of the system

Worm self-associating malicious code that distributes itself from one computer to another through network connections

Case Example

It was a bright, sunny afternoon and Paul was very happy. His term had ended, so he was on break from school for a few weeks. Paul loves music very much, so whenever he gets free time, he chills out listening to music. His favorite is country music, but Paul has a very limited selection of songs. He was getting bored listening to the same songs again and again, so he called Jack, his neighborhood friend, to find out whether he had any MP3 CDs. Jack could not help Paul, but he gave him a tip about an online music site. According to Jack, the online music portal allowed users to download music of any genre.

Paul was very excited to know this. He logged on to his computer and accessed the Web site. To his surprise, he found many songs that he was interested in. Paul started downloading a few songs. After downloading a particular song, Paul's system prompted him for a restart, which he allowed. To his dismay, his computer did not boot up.

Paul was wondering what happened to his system. Can you think of what went wrong with Paul's computer? What would you have done in Paul's place?

Introduction

This chapter lays the groundwork for future topics by defining the terminology essential to understanding the concept of computer security. It also gives an overview of security, cyber crime, and the security process.

Essential Terminology

The essence of this section is to lay out a standard terminology to be used throughout the book. What does it mean to say that an exploit has occurred? To understand this concept, you need to understand what constitutes a threat and a vulnerability.

A *threat* is an indication of a potential undesirable event. It refers to a situation in which human or natural occurrences can cause an undesirable outcome. It has been variously defined in the current context as:

- An action or event that might prejudice security

- Sequences of circumstances and events that allow a human or other agent to cause an information-related misfortune by exploiting vulnerabilities in an IT product; a threat can be either *intentional* (e.g., intelligent, e.g., an individual cracker or a criminal organization) or *accidental* (e.g., the possibility of a computer malfunctioning, or the possibility of an act of God, such as an earthquake, a fire, or a tornado)

- Any circumstance or event with the potential to cause harm to a system in the form of destruction, disclosure, modification of data, or denial of service

- A potential for violation of security, which exists when there is a circumstance, capability, action, or event that could breach security and cause harm

- U. S. government usage: the technical and operational capability of a hostile entity to detect, exploit, or subvert friendly information systems and the demonstrated, presumed, or inferred intent of that entity to conduct such activity

This brings us to discussing the term *vulnerability*. **Vulnerability** has been variously defined in the current context as:

- A security weakness in a target of evaluation (e.g., due to failures in analysis, design, implementation, or operation)
- Weakness in an information system or components (e.g., system security procedures, hardware design, or internal controls) that could be exploited to produce an information-related misfortune
- The existence of a weakness, design, or implementation error that can lead to an unexpected, undesirable event compromising the security of the system, network, application, or protocol involved

It is important to note the difference between threat and vulnerability because, inherently, most systems have vulnerabilities of some sort. However, this does not mean that the systems are too flawed for usability. The key difference between threat and vulnerability is that not every threat results in an attack, and not every attack succeeds. Success depends on the degree of vulnerability, the strength of attacks, and the effectiveness of any countermeasures in use. If the attacks needed to exploit vulnerability are very difficult to carry out, then the vulnerability may be tolerable.

If the perceived benefit to an attacker is small, then even an easily exploited vulnerability may be tolerable. However, if the attacks are well understood and easily made, and if the vulnerable system is employed by a wide range of users, then it is likely that there will be enough benefit for the perpetrator to make an attack.

Logically, the next essential term is **attack**. What is being attacked here? The information resource that is being protected and defended against attacks is referred to as the **target of evaluation**. The resource could be an IT system, product, or component that is identified as requiring security evaluation.

An attack is defined as an assault on system security that derives from an intelligent threat, which is an *intelligent* act that is a *deliberate attempt* (especially in the sense of a method or technique) to evade security services and violate the security policy of a system.

Attacks can be broadly classified as active and passive:

- *Active attacks* are those that modify the target system or message; attacks that violate the integrity of the system or message are examples of an active attack. Another example in this category is an attack on the availability of a system or service, a so-called denial-of-service (DoS) attack. Active attacks can affect the system in terms of its **availability**, which is the ability to use the information or resource as desired; **integrity**, which is the trustworthiness of data or resources in terms of preventing improper and unauthorized changes; and **authenticity**, which is the identification and assurance of the origin of information.
- *Passive attacks* are those that violate confidentiality without affecting the state of the system. An example of a passive attack is electronic eavesdropping on network transmissions to gather message contents or unprotected passwords. The key word here is **confidentiality**, which relates to preventing the disclosure of information to unauthorized persons.

The difference between these categories is that while an active attack attempts to alter system resources or affect their operation, a passive attack attempts to learn or make use of information from the system but does not affect system resources. Attacks can also be categorized as originating from within the organization or external to it.

- *An inside attack* is initiated by an entity inside the security perimeter (an insider); an entity that is authorized to access system resources but uses them in a way not approved by those granting the authority.
- *An outside attack* is initiated from outside the perimeter, by an unauthorized or illegitimate user of the system (an outsider). Potential outside attackers can range from amateur pranksters to organized criminals, international terrorists, or hostile governments.

How does an attack agent (or attacker) take advantage of the vulnerability of the system? The act of taking advantage of system vulnerability is termed an *exploit*. An **exploit** is a defined way to breach the security of an IT system through vulnerability.

What comprises a breach of security will vary from one organization to another or even from one department to another. This variability is why it is imperative for organizations to address both penetration and protection issues. The scope of this book is limited to the penetration aspect (ethical hacking); while the organization (company or department within a company) must address the protection issues through security policies and ensure that it complies with the requirements of a security audit. When a threat is exploited, it can be exposed. However, not every exposure is vulnerability. *Exposure* can be defined as a security violation that results from a threat action. Exposure includes disclosure, deception, disruption, and usurpation. An exposure is the primary entry point an attacker can use to gain increased access to the system or to data. It allows an attacker to conduct information gathering and then hide those activities.

What Is Security?

Security is a state of stability of information and infrastructure in which the possibility of successful yet undetected theft, tampering, and disruption of information and services is kept low or tolerable.

Note: Total protection is not required, as that is not practically possible considering the evolution of technology and the dynamic environment of the system. "The network is the computer" is a phrase coined by Sun Microsystems in the mid-1980s, which is even truer today.

There are several aspects to security in the current context. The owner of a system should have confidence that the system will behave according to its specifications, which is known as *assurance*. Systems, users, and applications need to interact with each other in a networked environment. Identification or authentication is a means to ensure security in such a scenario. System administrators, or another authority, need to know who has accessed the system resources when, where and for what purpose. An audit trail or log files can address this aspect of security, which is termed accountability. Not all resources are usually available to all users. This practice can have strategic implications. Having access controls on predefined parameters can help achieve these security requirements.

Another security aspect, critical at the systems operational level, is reusability. Objects used by one process may not be reused or manipulated by another process such that security may be violated, which is known as availability in security parlance. Information and processes need to be accurate in order to derive value from the system resource. Accuracy is a key security element. The aspects discussed previously constitute the integrity of the system.

Need for Security

Today, organizations are rapidly linked together through the exchange of information, creating multiple interwoven networks. Information is exchanged almost as fast as we think it. Routine tasks rely on the use of computers for accessing, providing, or just storing information. However, as information assets differentiate the competitive organization from others of its kind, so do they register an increase in their contribution to corporate capital. There is a sense of urgency on behalf of the organization to secure these assets from likely threats and vulnerabilities. The subject of addressing information security is vast, and it is the goal of this book to give students a comprehensive body of knowledge required to secure the information assets under their protection.

This book assumes that organizational policies exist that are endorsed by the top-level management and that business objectives and goals related to security have been incorporated as part of the corporate strategy. A security policy is the specification of how objects in a security domain are allowed to interact. To begin with, we shall briefly highlight the need to address the security concerns in the contemporary business world.

The importance of security in the information and communication technologies (ICT) world cannot be overemphasized. There are many reasons for securing ICT infrastructure. For our discussion here, we shall take a macro-level view. The evolution of computers has moved from mainframe computers at universities to personal-use laptops and PDAs. Initially, computers were designed to facilitate research, which did not place much emphasis on security as these resources, being scarce, were meant for sharing. The spread of computers into the workplace and daily life has led to more control being transferred to computers and a higher dependency on them for facilitating important routine tasks. Any disruption means loss of time, money, and sometimes life.

Cyber Crime

Cyber crime is defined as any illegal act involving a computer, its systems, or its applications and the Internet. Cyber crimes can be broadly separated into two categories:

1. *Crimes facilitated by a computer*: Computer-facilitated crime occurs when a computer is used as a tool to aid criminal activity. This category includes storing fraudulent records, producing false identification, reproducing and distributing copyrighted material, collecting and distributing child pornography.

2. *Crimes where the computer is the target*: Crimes where computers are the targets are not similar to traditional types of crimes. Sophisticated technology has made it more difficult to answer questions about identification of the criminal, nature of the crime, identity of the victim, location or jurisdiction of the crime, and other details; therefore, in an electronic or digital environment, evidence has to be collected and handled differently than at a traditional crime scene.

Information Security Statistics

The Cyber Security Enhancement Act 2002 mandates life sentences for hackers who "recklessly" endanger the lives of others. The CSI/FBI 2002 Computer Crime and Security Survey noted that 90% of the respondents acknowledged security breaches but only 34% reported the crime to law enforcement agencies. One reason for this disparity is the stigma associated with reporting security lapses. The FBI computer crimes squad estimates that between 85% and 97% of computer intrusions are not even detected.

The information security budget allocations in 2004 were higher than the previous year. IT security budgets rose from $5 million to an average of $7.3 million in the year 2004.

Security, Functionality, and the Ease-Of-Use Triangle

Technology is evolving at an unprecedented rate, and as a result, the products that reach the market are engineered more for ease of use than for secure computing. Technology originally developed for research work and campus-related work has not evolved entirely at the pace with which the user profile and span has; however, increasing built-in default security mechanisms means users have to be more competent. Moreover, vulnerabilities are often overlooked by system designers and remain unnoticed through the intended deployment of the system.

Because applications by default are preconfigured for ease of use, they are more vulnerable to security lapses. Increased functionality in any software product is a matter of concern—especially when the end user is unaware of the vulnerabilities associated with that functionality. Unfortunately, moving toward security means moving away from functionality and ease of use. Figure 1-1 illustrates this ease-of-use triangle.

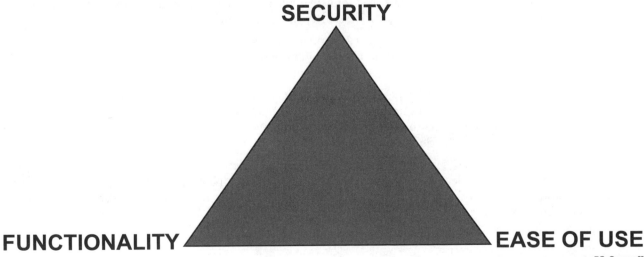

Figure 1-1 The ease-of-use triangle illustrates the relationship between security, functionality, and ease of use. As security increases, functionality and/or ease of use decreases.

As computers gain greater control over routine activities, it is becoming increasingly difficult for system administrators and other system professionals to allocate resources exclusively for securing systems. This allocation includes time needed to check log files, detect vulnerabilities, and sometimes apply security update patches.

The time available to system administrators is consumed by routine activities with less time available for vigilant administration. There is too little time at hand to deploy, measure, and secure computing resources on a regular and innovative basis. This situation has increased the demand for dedicated security professionals who will constantly monitor and defend the ICT resources.

Originally, *to hack* meant to possess extraordinary computer skills used to extend the limits of computer systems. It required great proficiency on the part of the individual; however, today there are automated tools and codes available on the Internet that make it possible for anyone with a will and desire to hack to succeed in their efforts.

Here, success need not denote the accomplishment of the objective. Mere compromise of the security of a system can denote success for the hacker. There are Web sites that insist on "taking back the net," as well as those who believe that they are doing all computer users a favor by hosting exploit details. Exposing these details is detrimental because it helps the novice hacker and reduces the skill level required to perpetrate the attack.

The ease with which system vulnerabilities can be exploited has increased while the knowledge curve required to perform such exploits is shortening. The concept of the elite super-hacker is as abstract as before. However, the fast-evolving genre of "script kiddies" largely consists of lesser-skilled individuals acquiring secondhand knowledge and performing exploits.

One of the main impediments to the growth of security infrastructure lies in the unwillingness of exploited or compromised victims to report the incident, for fear of losing the goodwill and faith of their employees, customers, and partners, and losing their market standing. The trend of market valuation being influenced by information assets has seen more enterprises think twice before reporting to law enforcement for fear of bad press and negative publicity.

The increasingly networked environment, with organizations often having their Web site as a single point of contact across geographical boundaries, makes it critical to take countermeasures to ward off any exploits that can result in loss—all the more reason why corporations should invest in security measures and protect their information assets.

Security Myths

The following are a few myths of information security:

1. *Security is a one-stage process*: Implementing information security policy in an organization is not an easy task. During the process of implementation, people within the organization may face many hindrances due to sudden changes in policies. Implementation of security policy cannot be stopped at one stage because as the organization grows, the need for new applications/systems/services increases, which in turn triggers a need for a revised security policy. Security must constantly be evaluated and revised.

2. *Increased spending hardens security*: Information security managers benchmark certain products to justify their security spending without looking into whether there is a real need for the product. This type of act only increases the expense but does not answer the genuine security needs of the firm.

3. *Software flaws cannot be avoided*: The majority of loopholes in applications, which in turn lure the attackers, are due to certain flaws in software. If software applications were properly tested, and all bugs or potential holes allowing unauthorized access were corrected, the attackers would have a difficult time in exploiting the applications.

4. *An external threat is a more serious concern than an internal one*: Statistics reveal that more than 80% of the reported incidents are internal attacks. Disgruntled employees are of serious concern to organizations and can lead to the threat of insider attacks. In this case, external perimeter defenses, such as firewalls, IDS, honeypots, fail to detect any attacks.

How to Harden Security

Creating security awareness within the organization or interacting within a peer group will lay a strong foundation for security. Most organizations do not consider security spending a major part of their annual plan. For some organizations, one-time security spending is more than sufficient. Following are some examples of system hardening.

One can secure computer, data, or e-mail clients by using strong passwords. Passwords that are a minimum of eight characters and are a combination of letters, numbers, and alphanumeric values are considered to be strongest.

While surfing on the Internet, users should be very cautious about clicking any unknown links, saving files without scanning, or downloading authentic software from third-party sites. There is a high chance of the system getting infected by a virus, worm, or Trojan horse if the protocol of safe browsing is not followed. A *virus* is malicious code written with the intention to damage the victim's computer. A *worm* is self-associating malicious code that distributes itself from one computer to another through network connections. A *Trojan horse* is a program that seems to be useful or harmless but contains hidden code embedded to take advantage of or damage the computer on which it is run. All of these threats fall under the category of *malware*, which is any software designed to infiltrate or damage a computer without the user's knowledge or consent.

Organizations have security policies that define the way internal communication is done, how the data is handled, which services are allowed to run in the LAN environment, and the logging actions. Security implementation is an ongoing process, so security policies should be implemented in phases.

Some Web sites list rogue IP addresses for the benefit of the Internet community. These IP addresses get blacklisted based on their activities on the Internet. To be safer, it is good policy to use information from such sites and block the blacklisted IP addresses.

Chapter Summary

- Understanding the terminology of information security is essential to learning about the security process.
- Security is a state of stability of information and infrastructure in which the possibility of successful yet undetected theft, tampering, and disruption of information and services is kept low or tolerable.
- As the prevalence of computers has increased, so has the need for security.
- Security is critical across sectors and industries.
- Cyber crime is any illegal act involving a computer, its systems, or its applications and the Internet; cyber crime can cover crimes facilitated by a computer or crimes where the computer is the target.
- IT security budget (sic) rose from $5 million to an average of $7.3 million in the year 2004.
- The ease-of-use triangle illustrates the relationship between security, functionality, and ease of use. As security increases, functionality and ease of use decrease.
- Security implementation is a continuous process and not a one-stage process.
- Increased spending alone will not harden security.
- Software applications need to be properly tested to cut down on vulnerability.
- More than 80% of attacks are internal.
- Companies and organizations should implement security policies and make sure they are followed.

Review Questions

1. How would you define *security*, as it was used in this chapter?

2. What is the difference between an attack and a threat?

3. Which type of threat—external or internal—is more of a risk for most organizations?

_____

_____

_____

_____

4. List and describe the categories of attack.

_____

_____

_____

_____

5. What is a vulnerability?

_____

_____

_____

_____

6. Is the budget allocated to fighting cyber crime increasing or decreasing? Describe why this is so.

_____

_____

_____

_____

7. What does the ease-of-use triangle say about functionality and security of software?

_____

_____

_____

_____

8. List and discuss two security myths discussed in the chapter.

_____

_____

_____

_____

9. What are some steps that can be taken to harden security?

_____

_____

_____

_____

10. What is cyber crime?

_____

_____

_____

_____

11. What are the two categories of cyber crime?

_____

_____

_____

_____

Hands-On Projects

1. Visit *www.cybercrime.gov* to get a better understanding of the facts and figures of cyber crime and other related articles.

2. Visit *www.securityfocus.com* to get comfortable with security-related issues.

3. Visit *www.webopedia.com*, an online dictionary, to look for terms related to computers and the Internet.

4. Visit *www.cert.org* to get up-to-date facts and figures of attacks and threats against computers and related news.

5. These Web sites cater to the area of information security:

   www.searchsecurity.com

   www.securiteam.com

   www.microsoft.com/security

   https://www.securityforum.org

   www.usdoj.gov

Chapter 2

Basic Security Procedures

Objectives

After completing this chapter, you should be able to:

- Appreciate the importance of security in daily routines
- Understand how to harden your operating system and deploy patches
- Configure update schedules for your operating system
- Disable unnecessary services
- Create strong passwords
- Disable guest account access
- Convert folders into "private" folders
- Understand macro security settings in common Microsoft Office applications

Key Terms

Antivirus software   programs that attempt to recognize the existence of, prevent the installation of, and remove computer viruses and other malicious software from the computer

Authentication   a method that ensures that the individual is who he or she claims to be by comparing the login name and password to the information stored in a database; authentication is granted if they match

Critical update   security patches that are made available to close security vulnerabilities that can allow a malicious user to access the system

Firewall   scheme designed to guard the system from unwarranted traffic by avoiding unauthorized access to or from a private network

Identification   users must initially identify themselves as valid users; this is usually done with a login or account name to ensure the users are who they claim to be

Malicious code   code that is deliberately incorporated in software or hardware for an unauthorized purpose

Password   a series of characters that enables the user to access a file, computer, or program

Password cracking   action taken by a malicious programmer, using specially designed software to guess or decrypt user passwords, who wants to break into computer systems to destroy, damage, or steal data

Patch   a short set of instructions to correct a bug in a computer program

Patching   reinstalling an updated installation package or applying a Windows Installer patch

Personal information   information collected that applies to a person (or corporation) and would be considered private

Update   a fix for a precise setback, tackling a noncritical, nonsecurity-related bug

Case Example

Jean has recently purchased a personal computer. She gets it preinstalled with MS Windows XP home edition and has purchased other software she would need. Jean is eager to connect to the Internet and access her e-mail. She connects to the ISP and when online, begins chatting with a friend. Approximately an hour later, she finds her machine responding erratically and it restarts on its own.

- What do you think went wrong with Jean's system?
- If you were in Jean's place, what would be the steps you would adopt to proactively secure your system?

During winter most of us are huddled in warm clothes. It is a precaution we take against the cold weather. Similarly, when you connect to the Internet, you need to take some precautions to protect your computer resources against intruders and misuse.

Introduction

This chapter explains some of the basic security procedures or practices one can adopt to address security proactively. The goal is to take charge of the security settings on your personal computer.

Why You Should Worry About Computer Security

Unlike in corporate networks where a systems administrator defends the network from the Internet to a great extent, a regular computer user in small office or home environments needs to have a greater awareness of security. Typically, a home computer is a much-sought-after target for hackers because hackers target the personal information stored in the computer and the computing resources.

For example, a hacker might be interested in personal information stored in your system or be looking at your 60GB hard disk and high-speed internet access to store illegal material for redistribution. *Personal information* is information collected that applies to a person (or corporation) and would be considered private, and it includes credit card numbers, bank account information, and anything else that can be used by hackers to sell or buy goods and services. Computing resources include hard disk space, a fast processor, and high-speed Internet connection. Hackers can use these resources to attack other computers on the Internet. Using other people's computers helps hackers leave a scattered trail of their activities, which makes it difficult for law enforcement to figure out the origin of the attack. If hackers cannot be traced, they cannot be apprehended and tried for their crimes.

Regular computer users are targeted more often than corporate networks because standalone computers are usually not very secure and therefore easier to break into. If these systems are connected to high-speed Internet access and are always turned on, hackers can easily seek them out and plan their illegal activities. Systems on dial-up connections are also vulnerable, but high-speed connections (cable modems and DSL modems) are preferred targets.

How do hackers attack a system? In some cases, they send the victim an e-mail with a virus. Reading that e-mail activates the virus and exposes a port of entry that hackers can use to enter or access the computer. In other cases, they take advantage of a flaw or weakness in one of the computer's programs—a vulnerability—to gain access.

Once inside the system, hackers often install new programs such as keystroke loggers or sniffers (eavesdropping software) that allow them to continue to use the system—even after the user addresses a vulnerability that exposed them to the hacker in the first place. These ports of reentry are usually cleverly disguised so that they blend in with the other programs running on the computer and remain undetected, especially in cases where original files are replaced by *malicious code,* which is code that is deliberately incorporated in software or hardware for an unauthorized purpose.

Following are examples of how to secure a Microsoft Windows 2000– or XP–based computer. The goal of this chapter is to educate you about security-related problems that you need to address.

Basic Security Practices

You might be a new user or a regular computer user who does normal day-to-day tasks. Whichever you are, you need to know the basic aspects of computer security. Security is an ongoing process, and all users need to be aware of certain basic security procedures and practices that can be followed to defend their systems. The key is to be proactive.

You can take a number of simple precautions to keep your digital personal information secure, including the following examples:

- If you have to store personal information on your machine, encrypt it.
- Use strong passwords.
- Keep your operating system and applications up to date and patched against the latest discovered vulnerabilities.
- Read Web site security and privacy policies.
- Always lock your system.
- Perform regular system backups to be able to restore your data.
- Never use confidential information on an instant messenger.
- Always exercise care with e-mail attachments.

Harden the Operating System

Every operating system or software application has some inherent flaws that are discovered after their adoption by users. Hackers seek out and use these flaws as a means to compromise a system. A vulnerability is the degree to which a software system or component is open to unauthorized access, change, or disclosure of information and is susceptible to interference or disruption of system services.

A *patch* is a short set of instructions to correct a bug in a computer program. Most users would agree that patching software with the latest fixes for vulnerabilities is essential. *Patching* is reinstalling an updated installation package or applying a Windows Installer patch; however, for patch management to be effective, the process should be easy to follow and maintained for timely response. Patch management ensures that all systems using particular software are closest to the latest configuration. Next, we will look at applying *updates* (a fix for a precise setback, tackling a noncritical, nonsecurity-related bug) to the Windows operating system and harden it against intruders and malicious code.

Following, you will see how you can apply the most current updates to your system when you connect to the Internet for the first time. After you have connected your computer to the Internet, it is important that you download and install the *critical updates*. These updates serve to close security vulnerabilities that can allow a malicious user to access the system.

Users of all versions of the Microsoft Windows operating system can visit Microsoft's Windows Update Web site *(http://windowsupdate.microsoft.com)*. This Web site will automatically take you to the correct set of updates for your computer's version of the Windows operating system. (Note: You must use Internet Explorer to use the Windows Update site.)

Microsoft never sends patches by e-mail. Sending fake patches by e-mail can be a hacker's way of conning you to install a malicious code and accessing your system. Always discard e-mail claiming to be from Microsoft with attached Windows patches. However, Microsoft does provide an e-mail alert service informing subscribers when security updates are released and refers users to the standard Microsoft update procedures.

The directions following show you how to apply updates for the first time for the Windows XP and 2000 operating systems.

1. In order for Windows Update to function properly, the date and time settings on the system need to be current. Before running Windows Update for the first time, check your computer's date setting to be sure it is accurate.

   *How to do this: Right-click on the clock in the computer's toolbar and then select **Adjust Date/Time**. You can also get there by clicking **Start -> Control Panel -> Date and Time**. Set the date and time if necessary. Click OK.*

2. Click on the computer's **Start** button.

3. Select **Windows Update**. (If the Start menu is displayed in "classic" mode, Windows Update is on the main Start menu. If the Start menu is displayed using the default XP appearance, select **All Programs**; then select **Windows Update**.)

4. If prompted with a security warning, select **Yes**; Internet Explorer will start and take the user to the Windows Update site.

5. You can also choose to go directly to the Windows Update site by typing *http://windowsupdate.microsoft. com* in your browser's address bar.

6. Select **Scan for Updates**. The site will scan your system to determine which updates are available for your particular version and configuration of the operating system.

7. Select **Review and Install Updates** to install the critical updates. There may be multiple critical updates. You can choose to download all or one at a time, depending on your Internet speed. If you choose single-update installation, repeat the process until you see this message: "There are no critical updates available at this time."

8. Select **Install Now**. After reviewing the Microsoft license agreement, select **Accept**. While the critical updates are being downloaded and installed, a progress bar will be displayed.

9. Upon completion, select **OK** when prompted to restart your system. The system will reboot with the critical updates installed.

Figure 2-1 reviews the previous steps.

Configuring Automatic Updates

As mentioned previously, patch management is an ongoing process and needs to be relatively easy to maintain, so that it is done in a timely manner. To keep the system protected on an ongoing basis, the user can activate Automatic Updates (Figure 2-2):

1. Select the **Start** button, and then select **Control Panel**.

2. Select **System**. Choose the **System** tab and choose **Automatic Updates**.

Source: www.microsoft.com

Figure 2-1   Updating the first time.

Source: www.microsoft.com

Figure 2-2   Configuring automatic updates.

If the control panel is displayed in "Classic View," you can go directly to the System window as shown above. Alternatively, if the system has Windows 2000 Service Pack 3 or higher, there is an icon labeled Automatic Updates in the Control Panel. Double-clicking this icon can help you schedule the updates.

*If the control panel is displayed in "Category View," select the **Performance and Maintenance** category, then select **System**, and then select the **Automatic Updates** tab.*

Automatic
Updates

3. In the dialog window, check the box next to **Keep my computer up to date**. With this setting enabled, Windows Update software may be automatically updated prior to applying any other updates.

4. In the **Settings** pane, select the third option **Automatically download the updates, and install them on the schedule that I specify**.

5. Choose **Every Day** and set a time of day when the computer is generally turned on and connected to the Internet. The computer will automatically check for updates at that time every day and install them as necessary. This is the recommended method.

6. Click **OK** when you are finished.

Figure 2-3 illustrates steps 3–6.

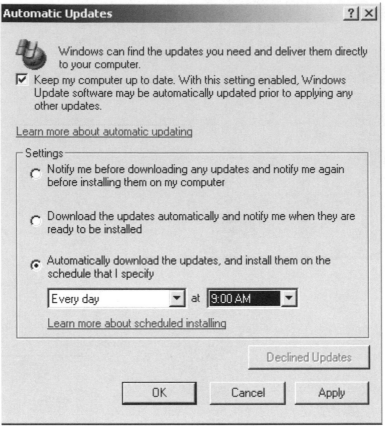

Figure 2-3 Automatic updates.

Pointers for Updates

Following are some pointers that you need to bear in mind when applying patches. Vendors often provide free patches on their Web sites. When you purchase programs, it is a good idea to see if and how the vendor supplies patches, and how they support their products. Always patch your operating system and applications to the latest patch levels. The longer a vulnerability is known, the greater the chances are that an intruder will find it and exploit it. Use automatic updates or patch management tools, if possible. Some vendors provide programs bundled with their systems that automatically contact their Web sites looking for patches. These automatic updates tell you when patches are available, download them, and even install them.

Most vendors provide patches on their site that are supposed to fix bugs in their products. Ensure that you download the patch directly from the vendor site, as other sources may be suspect. Program vendors also provide a recall-like service. You can receive patch notices through e-mail by subscribing to mailing lists operated by the programs' vendors. Through this type of service, you can learn about problems with your computer even before you discover them and, hopefully, before intruders have the chance to exploit them. Consult the vendor's Web site to see how to get e-mail notices about patches as soon as they're available.

Disable Unnecessary Services

Services are small programs that run in the background and perform many essential operations for servers and workstations. During a normal default installation of the Windows operating system, several services are installed and activated during the boot process by default. A major security issue for any system is running unneeded services in the background that can open holes for attackers to gain access.

Many of these services are unnecessary and can be turned off safely without any concern of limiting the computing needs of a common user. Some services have had security problems or flaws previously that have allowed hackers and malicious code to take advantage of them and use them as ports of entry into

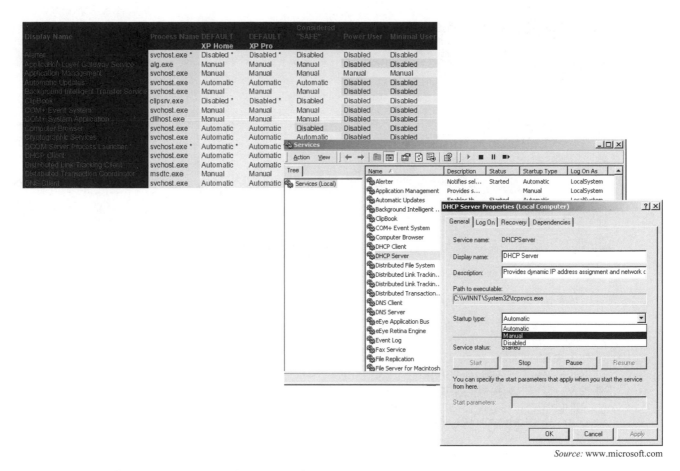

Source: www.microsoft.com

Figure 2-4 Disabling services in Windows XP and 2000.

unsuspecting machines. By shutting down unneeded services, common users can close security holes and recover system resources.

The following shows how to disable these services:

1. Click **Start**.
2. Choose **Control Panel**.
3. Choose **Administrative Tools**.
4. Choose **Services**.
5. Right-click on the desired service; choose **Properties** and apply desired settings.

Figure 2-4 shows (in the first screen) some services with their default settings in XP Home and Pro. The desired setting for a power user and minimal or normal user is also shown. The next screens show services being checked in Windows 2000.

How a User Knows What Services Are Needed

Guides are available from the vendor or from reliable sites that state which services are required for a particular type of user. See the PDF document in the Appendix for essential services in Windows XP. Table 2-1 shows an excerpt from this document.

Use Strong Passwords

When you access a protected resource, you are asked "Who are you?" and "Are you who you claim to be?" These are the two essential components to secure authorized access to an information resource: *identification*—users must initially identify themselves as valid users, usually with a login or account name to ensure users are

Service	Process	XP Pro	XP Home	"Safe"	Power User	Minimal User
Distributed Link Tracking Client	svchost.exe	Automatic	Automatic	Manual	Disabled	Disabled
Distributed Transaction Coordinator	msdtc.exe	Manual	Manual	Manual	Disabled	Disabled
DNS Client	svchost.exe	Automatic	Automatic	Automatic	Disabled	Disabled
Error Reporting Service	svchost.exe	Automatic	Automatic	Disabled	Disabled	Disabled
Event Log	services.exe	Automatic	Automatic	Automatic	Automatic	Automatic
Fast User Switching Compatibility	svchost.exe	Manual	Manual	Manual	Disabled	Disabled
Fax	fxssvc.exe	Not Installed	Not Installed	Not Installed	Not Installed	Not Installed

Table 2-1   Excerpt of essential services in Windows XP

who they claim to be—and *authentication*—a method that ensures the individual is who he or she claims to be by comparing the login name and password to the information stored in a database; authentication is granted if they match.

Passwords, a series of characters that enables the user to access a file, computer, or program, are a simple means of ensuring the authentication aspect of secure access. Passwords are typically case sensitive (they recognize both lowercase and uppercase letters). They are much sought after by attackers trying to gain unauthorized access to information and resources.

A strong password is one that is difficult to detect by both humans and computer programs; one that effectively protects data from unauthorized access. A strong password consists of at least seven characters (the more characters, the stronger the password will be). They should ideally be a combination of letters, numbers and symbols (@, #, $, %, etc.). Symbols are not always allowed in passwords. Strong passwords also do not contain words that can be found in a dictionary or parts of the user's own name, as this is easily guessed by the attacker.

Attackers can use tools such as password crackers that can check for a match from a list of words in a dictionary or try a combination of letters and words to forcefully attack the password-protected resource. Strong passwords need not be difficult to remember and can be easily drawn from daily life. Following is an illustration of how to create a strong password.

Jason decides to use the name of a song for his password. He chooses "She will be loved" by Maroon 5. Let us see how he goes about developing a strong password when he knows that this song can be on a music-based **password**-cracking dictionary (*password cracking* is action taken by a malicious programmer, using specially designed software to guess or decrypt user passwords, who wants to break into computer systems to destroy, damage, or steal data):

- First he takes the second letters of all the words in the title. "h," "i," "e," and "o."
- Then he alternates upper and lower case. "H," "i," "E," and "o."
- Now he takes the name of the artist. He substitutes "oo" as "8" and "a" as "1." He also chooses the "5" in the band's name.
- He then alternates the numbers with the letters: H 1 i 8 E 5 o.
- His password is now "H1i8E5o."

Try a simple example with a nursery rhyme or a favorite song of yours. Always remember that passwords need to be changed frequently. Do not write down the passwords in areas where others can see it. Be careful when you type your passwords so that nobody peeping over your shoulder can guess them easily.

Deploy Antivirus Software and a Firewall

Antivirus software can help a user detect the existence of malicious code and remove it from the infected system. By installing an antivirus program, a user can also prevent virus infections, as the software can be used to scan any program or document before it is opened. Antivirus programs can also be used to check e-mails and

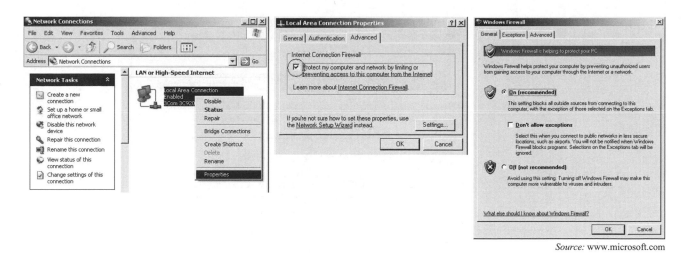

Source: www.microsoft.com

Figure 2-5   Windows XP Firewall.

e-mail attachments before they are read. An antivirus program must be constantly updated to include new virus signatures and virus definitions. The antivirus software works by checking files for the virus signatures it has stored, thereby protecting them from infection.

Configure the antivirus to scan the system regularly and set the virus definition (DAT) files to autoupdate

A *firewall* is a software or hardware scheme that guards the system from unwarranted traffic when it is connected to a network. Hackers can try to take advantage of programs running on the system and try to execute malicious code. Hacking tools such as Trojan horses can send information from the victim's computer to the attacker's computer. A firewall can detect this activity and can allow the user to block certain traffic or programs that need not access network resources. Even firewalls need to have their "rules" updated so that they can prevent illegitimate traffic. A firewall that "learns" is one where the user is asked for permitting or blocking traffic when a program tries to access the network initially. The firewall then enforces the rule for every other instance of the program.

Use a firewall that will learn the rules as you operate so that you can ensure what resources access the Internet and what is accessed over the Internet.

Popular antivirus and firewall programs include Norton Antivirus, McAfee Personal Firewall, and Norton Internet Security.

Here are the steps to turn on the XP Internet Connection Firewall (Figure 2-5):

1. Click **Start**, and then click **Control Panel**.

2. Click **Network and Internet Connections**.

3. Click **Network Connections**.

4. Highlight a connection that you want to help protect, and then click **Change settings of this connection**. Alternatively, right-click the connection, and click **Properties**.

5. Click **Advanced**, and then select **Protect my computer and network by limiting or preventing access to this computer from the Internet**.

6. Click **OK**.

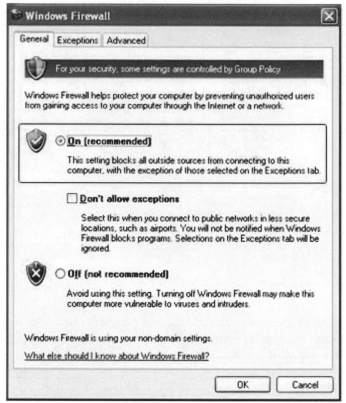

Figure 2-6   Windows Firewall settings.

The Windows XP Internet Connection Firewall might prevent the user from performing useful tasks, such as sharing files or printers on a network, using instant messaging (IM), or hosting multiplayer computer games. You can choose to allow these types of activities by adding them to the exception list (Figure 2-6):

1. Click **Start** and then click **Control Panel**.
2. In the control panel, click **Security Center,** and then click **Windows Firewall**.
3. On the **Exceptions** tab, under Programs and Services, select the check box for the program or service that you want to allow, and then click OK.

If the program (or service) to be allowed is not listed:

1. Click **Add Program**.
2. In the **Add a Program** dialog box, click the program that you want to add, and then click **OK**. The program will appear, selected, on the **Exceptions** tab, under Programs and Services.

Disable Guest Accounts

You should also disable any guest accounts on the system because they can provide information to intruders and increase the security risk.

To disable guest accounts in Windows XP (Figure 2-7):

1. Click the **Start** button in the lower left corner of the desktop.
2. Click **Settings,** and then click **Control Panel**.
3. Click **User Accounts**.
4. In the User Accounts window, click **Guest**.
5. Click **Turn off the guest account**.

To disable guest accounts in Windows 2000 (Figure 2-8):

1. Click the **Start** button in the lower left corner of the desktop.
2. Click **Settings,** and then click **Control Panel.**
3. Click **Users and Passwords.**
4. Click the **Advanced** tab.
5. In the **Advanced User Management** dialog, click **Advanced.**
6. In the **Local Users and Groups** dialog, click the **Users** folder.
7. Right-click the **Guest** account, and select **Properties.**

Source: www.microsoft.com

Figure 2-7   Disable guest accounts in Windows XP.

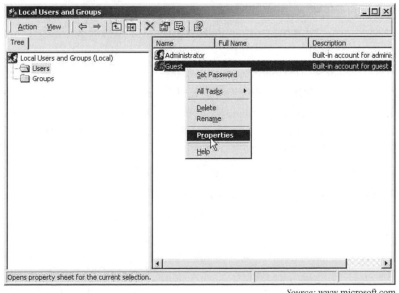

Source: www.microsoft.com

Figure 2-8   Disable guest accounts in Windows 2000.

8. Select the **Account is Disabled** check box.

9. Click **Apply**.

Make Folders Private

The option to make folders private is only available for folders included in the user profile, which is used to store information and items associated with a particular user. Folders in the user profile include My Documents and its subfolders, Desktop, Start Menu, Cookies, and Favorites. If these folders are not made private, they will be available to everyone who uses the computer. When a folder is made private, all of its subfolders are private as well. For example, when My Documents is made private, My Music and My Pictures are rendered private too. Follow these steps to make folders private:

1. Click **Start** and then **My Computer**.

2. Double-click the drive where the Windows operating system is installed (usually drive C:).

3. Double-click the **Documents and Settings** folder.

4. Double-click your user folder.

5. Right-click any folder in your user profile, and then click **Properties**.

6. On the **Sharing** tab, select the **Make this folder private (so that only you have access to it)** check box.

In the MS Windows operating systems, there are almost always multiple ways to accomplish the same task. Here is another option:

1. Right-click the folder that you want to make private and choose **Properties**.

2. Go to the **Sharing** tab and check the **Make this folder private** box.

Security Settings in Microsoft Office Applications

The term *macro* includes any executable file that can be attached to a document, worksheet, e-mail message, etc., for Word, Excel, or PowerPoint. Macros are normally used to map a short string of characters to a longer sequence or set of instructions. For Outlook, Microsoft Publisher, and Microsoft FrontPage, the term *macro* is explicitly used for macros used by Visual Basic for Applications. Macro security levels can be low, medium or high. Macros can be unsigned, signed (a digital signature is an encrypted value used to ensure identity and integrity) and from a trusted source, or signed from an unknown source.

The security levels for unsigned macros are

- High—Macros are disabled, and the document, workbook, presentation, or e-mail message is opened.

- Medium—User is prompted to enable or disable macros.

The security levels for signed macros from a trusted source with a valid certificate are

- High and Medium—Macros are enabled, and the document, workbook, presentation, or e-mail message is opened.

The security levels for signed macros from an unknown source with a valid certificate, which is a digital certificate that is the verification by an authority of the identity, are

- High and Medium—A dialog box appears with information about the certificate; users must then determine whether they should enable any macros based on the content of the certificate. To enable the macros, users must accept the certificate.

To set the security level in Word, Excel, or PowerPoint (Figure 2-9):

1. On the Tools menu, point to **Macro**, and then click **Security**.

2. Click the **Security Level** tab, and then select a security level.

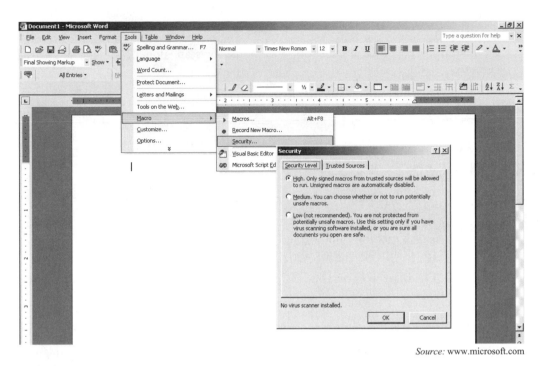

Source: www.microsoft.com

Figure 2-9   Setting the security level in Word, Excel, or PowerPoint.

Chapter Summary

- Use strong passwords.
- Always install security patches for both your operating system and applications.
- Set up automatic installation of patches for timely application.
- Install and always update antivirus software.
- Activate or install a software firewall.
- Disable unnecessary accounts and services.
- Use private folders.

Review Questions

1. It is necessary to patch applications even if the operating system is _____.

2. Running all services does not compromise security if _____ is installed.

3. Hackers target home (or standalone) computers for the user's _____ and for the computer's _____.

4. Hackers target home (or standalone) computers because they are not as _____ as corporate (or networked) computers.

5. Microsoft never sends patches by _____.

6. Using _____ is the best way to make sure you have current security patches for your operating system and software applications.

7. A major security issue for any system is running unneeded _____ in the background.

8. A strong password consists of at least _____ characters.

9. Passwords are typically _____ senstitive.

10. Another strategy to increase security on a home (or standalone) computer is to disable _____ accounts.

11. Making a folder private means that its contents cannot be _____.

12. Macros can be _____, signed and from a trusted source, or signed from an unknown source.

Hands-On Projects

1. Visit *http://windowsupdate.microsoft.com*. Familiarize yourself with the update site. If feasible, connect your system to the site and scan your system for updates.

2. Configure automatic update for every Friday at 3 a.m. on your system. Or pick a time when the computer is least likely to be in use but is turned on.

3. Open services on your system and disable "Error Reporting Service."

4. Check if the guest account on your system is disabled.

5. What is the antivirus software installed on your system? Configure it for automatic updates.

6. Explore the XP firewall and activate security logging. Consider turning the firewall and logging features on if you do not have one already installed on your system.

Desktop Security

Objectives

After completing this chapter, you should be able to:

- Share files
- Hide files
- Transfer and download files
- Back up and restore data
- Encrypt and decrypt files
- Lock your workstation
- Use Task Manager to kill suspicious processes
- Take precautions while downloading files and DLLs

Key Terms

Data restoration   restoring data that is lost, corrupted, or deleted either intentionally or unintentionally

Decryption   a type of file protection that decodes the data within an encrypted file

Default share   a method of file sharing that does not require any specific access permissions apart from the share designation

Dynamic Library Linked (DLL) files   used to combine multiple programs to give the appearance that a single program is running

Encryption   the process of camouflaging information in an attempt to make it secure from unauthorized access

File backup   a type of file safeguarding method that enables you to store copies of critical files and folders on another medium for safekeeping

File sharing   a network association between computers that allows them to share data

File transfer   the process of making use of communications between two computers or more to send a file between them

Keylogger   a program that records the keystrokes made by a user on a computer

Malicious dialer program   a type of spyware that can install itself to your dial-up settings to redirect Internet connections

Peer-to-Peer (P2P) applications   applications that run on your computer that allow you to directly connect to someone else's computer, and that person to yours, in order to transfer files back and forth

Process   a single executable element that runs concurrently with other executable elements

Process tree   displays the hierarchy in a tree structure of all the instances of a program being executed; programs are sets of instructions, and a process is the actual execution of those instructions

Restricted share   a method of file sharing that requires specific access permissions

Case Example

Jane has recently joined an equity research firm as a research assistant. Her job involves profiling corporate value and risk issues, and keeping investors informed about their choices. Because of the sensitive nature of her job, Jane must secure her desktop from unauthorized access and take needed precautions to secure her data.

What could Jane do to be sure that when she is away from her desk in a meeting, no one is looking at the data she has gathered? What can Jane do to protect the sensitive data on her laptop in case it is stolen while traveling?

Introduction

In this chapter, we will explore some of the challenges that arise in the workplace when it comes to securing computers and their files, and we will suggest ways to address these challenges.

File Sharing

Sharing data over a network is called *file sharing*. Once a file is shared on the network, it is called a *shared* file. The owner of the file can limit sharing access to other users accessing the file. Access to the shared file is sometimes regulated by password protection, account or security authorizations, or locking the file to avoid simultaneous changes from being made by more than one user at a time.

The term *file sharing* also refers to the users being allotted the same or different levels of access privilege. The files may be stored in a particular central system, also known as the server, and can be accessed by more than one user depending upon the levels of access privilege.

The user must keep the following points in mind while sharing a folder:

- Only folders can be shared—not files.

- Shared folders are only related to users who access the folder over a network. It does not apply to users who locally log on to the computer.

- When a copy of the shared folder is made, only the original shared folder is shared and not the copied one.

- When the shared folder is moved from its original position, the folder will lose its sharing.

Default Share

A *default share* is a method of folder sharing that would not require any specific access permissions apart from the share designation. These types of shares can be created locally or on a network. All users of the local machine can have access to the shared folder if the user sets a default local share. When the user sets a default network share in a workgroup setting, all users in the workgroup can access the files.

Restricted Share

A *restricted share* is a method of folder sharing that contains more restrictions than a default share. This type of share can be created locally or on a network. The user can restrict the number of users who can access the share at a particular given time. The user is also allowed to designate specific users who can access the share and allot permissions to control user activity on the share.

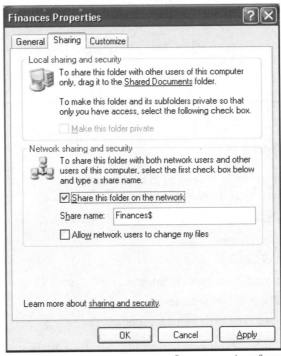

Source: www.microsoft.com

Figure 3-1   Sharing a folder.

How to Share a Folder

The following steps show how to share a folder (Figure 3-1):

1. Right-click the folder to be shared, and click **Properties.**
2. Click the **Sharing** tab in the folder's properties dialog box.
3. Click **Share this folder on the network,** and then in **Share name,** type the name of the share.
4. If the name given to the new share ends in a $, such as MyPrivateFolder$, the folder is shared, but the folder does not appear when users browse for it across the network.

- The shared folder permissions are set to the Everyone group with Full Control permission.
- The user can also share a folder from the command prompt by using the **net share** command.

5. In **Comment,** type a description for the shared folder. This description is visible to users who browse across the network.
6. In **User limit,** the user can make any changes required.
7. The default setting is **Maximum allowed,** which corresponds to the number of client access licenses you have purchased. The user can also designate a user limit by clicking **Allow,** typing the number of users next to **Users,** and then clicking **OK.**

Configuring Shared Folder Permissions

You can restrict access to your folders if someone's job status changes, so they no longer have access to your folders (e.g., they quit or move to another department). Follow these steps to restrict access to your folders:

1. Right-click the folder and click **Properties.**
2. In the folder's properties dialog box, click the **Sharing** tab, and then click **Permissions.**
3. In the **Permissions for** dialog box, click **Add.**

4. In the **Select Users, Computers, or Groups** dialog box, click **Object Types,** click the **Users** check box, and then click **OK.**

5. Under **Enter the object names to select,** type the name of the group or user for which permissions need to be configured, and then click **OK.**

6. In the **Permissions for** dialog box, in the **Group or user names box,** click the group or user.

7. In the **Permissions for** dialog box, allow or deny permissions, and then click **OK.**

Hiding Files and Folders

It is possible to add another level of protection in case an unauthorized person does gain access to your system. You can hide files and folders by following these steps (Figure 3-2):

1. Right-click the file or folder to be hidden and click **Properties.**
2. Under **Attributes,** check **Hidden.**
3. Click **Apply** and then click **OK.**
4. Select the **Tools** menu and click **Folder options.**
5. In the **View** tab, there is a list of options.
6. Select the **Do not show hidden files and folders** option.

This process completely hides the file or folder. The file or folder would become visible but faded only when the user selects **Show hidden files and folders** from Folder options.

Transferring Files

With the rise of file sharing networks and instant messenger, you need to be sure that you know how to transfer files safely. *File transfer* is the process of making use of communications between two computers or more to send a file between them. Files can be transferred in various ways. A file can be transferred via e-mail or messengers like Yahoo! and MSN. The user must be sure to scan the file for viruses or malware before and after acquiring or transferring the file. A file can also be transferred using FTP, Telnet, and Web folders. With these methods, the user must enter a valid user name and password for authorized access to transfer files. The password protection enhances the security because no other user can get access to the files stored at a particular FTP location.

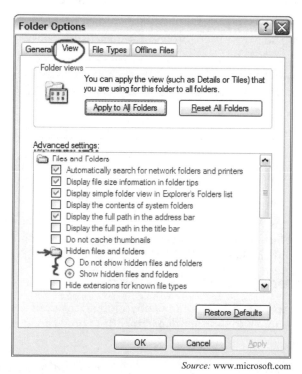

Source: www.microsoft.com

Figure 3-2 Hiding files and folders.

Files can also be transferred through peer-to-peer networks. There are numerous peer-to-peer applications (P2P) available on the Internet these days. *Peer-to-peer applications* run on your computer and allow you to directly connect to someone else's computer, and that person to yours, in order to transfer files back and forth. Some of them are Emule, BearShare, Warez, Morpheus, and Kazaa. These P2P applications are configured by default in such a way that all the members of the network can access each other's hard drives and folders. This default feature must be disabled by the user to securely download and upload files.

Downloading Files

File downloading is a common activity among computer users these days. Downloading a file from unknown or untrustworthy sources makes the computer vulnerable to many threats. It may not be safe to open a file or run a program directly from any particular download source. Saving the downloaded file in the root directory (commonly C:\) is risky. The downloaded file should be saved in any directory other than the root directory to keep the operating system files and program files safe. Saving the file before running or opening it allows the following precautions:

- The file can be scanned for viruses/malware using a virus scanner present in the system.
- The user can save all his other work and close other programs before opening the file.
- The user can also take a backup of all other data before opening the file.

File Backup

File backup is a type of file safeguarding method that enables you to store copies of critical files and folders on another medium for safekeeping. Backups protect against loss of data due to disasters such as file corruption or hardware failure. Information that you back up is static, so if additional changes are made to a file after the backup, the backup copy will not include the changes.

There are many different types of media on which you can store backed-up data, including a different hard disk, floppy disks, rewritable CD-ROMs, tape drives, and compact storage media such as jump drives. Windows offers several ways for you to back up your data. Deciding when and how to back up data depends on a number of issues. Selecting the correct backup options for your specific situation can help ensure that your information is properly protected from disaster.

How to Back Up a File

Follow these steps to back up files in Windows (Figures 3-3 and 3-4):

1. The user must check whether he/she is authorized to back up the file. Persons who can back up are:
   - System administrator or backup operator.
   - The owner of the file.
   - Users with permissions to back up the file.
2. Select **Backup** wizard.
   - **Start** menu -> **All programs** -> **Accessories** -> **System Tools** -> **Backup.**
3. Click **Next.**
   - **Backup files and settings** is selected by default.
4. Click **Next.**
   - **What to backup** window is shown.
5. Choose the required backup option and click **Next.** The user can also select the file and click **Next.**
   - The options are:
     - My documents and settings
     - Everyone's documents and settings
     - All information on this computer
     - Let me choose what to backup

Source: www.microsoft.com

Figure 3-3   Backup options.

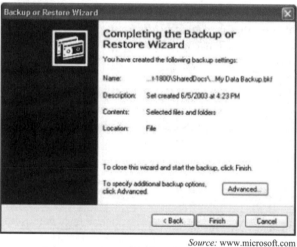

Source: www.microsoft.com

Figure 3-4   Backup or Restore wizard.

6. Choose the destination and backup file name and click **Next.**

   • If you wanted to back up data to your CD drive and call it "Backup01," the file destination would be D:\ and the file would be named "Backup01."

7. Click **Finish** to complete the wizard.

8. Review and close the report, if desired.

9. Click **Close** to close the **Backup** progress box.

Data Restoration

Data restoration is a type of information protection scheme that enables the user to recover stored copies of files and folders from another medium. Restores protect the user against loss of data due to disasters, and go hand in hand with data backups. Restored information will not include any changes made after the backup file was created.

Data restoration can be local or network-based. It can be accomplished in several ways, including manually copying individual files and folders from another location and using software specifically designed to assist the user in restoring data. Windows XP Professional also comes with recovery utilities called System Restore, Recovery Console, and Automated System Recovery.

How to Restore Data

These are the steps to restore data in Windows (Figure 3-5):

1. Select the **Backup or Restore** wizard.
   - **Start** menu -> **All programs** -> **Accessories** -> **System Tools** -> **Backup**
2. Click **Next.**
   - **Backup files and settings** is selected by default.
3. Select **Restore files and settings** and click **Next** to show the **What to restore** screen.
4. Select the file to be restored and click **Next.**
5. Review and close the report.
6. Click **Close** to exit the dialog box.

Encryption

Encryption protects data by camouflaging it within a file or message, so that unauthorized users cannot use it. File encryption is a type of file protection that disguises the data within a file or message so that the specific information included within the file or message cannot be read or understood by unauthorized users. A key is used to encode the data, and neither the file nor the key contents can be read by anyone who does not have the key. File encryption can be local, where a file that is on a disk is protected, or it can be used when a file is being transmitted over a network connection.

Windows Encrypting File System (EFS)

Windows EFS enables users to encrypt files that are stored on a Windows 2000 or XP computer that uses the NTFS file system. It does not work on compressed files or folders, or on system files or the system root (C:\Windows) folder. By default, the user who encrypted the file or folder can access the encrypted material transparently. Other users will be able to see the files and folders that are encrypted, but they will not be able to access the content of the files. A best practice is to encrypt the parent folder to protect any temporary and associated files.

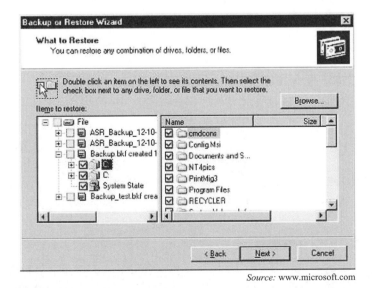

Source: www.microsoft.com

Figure 3-5   Restoring data.

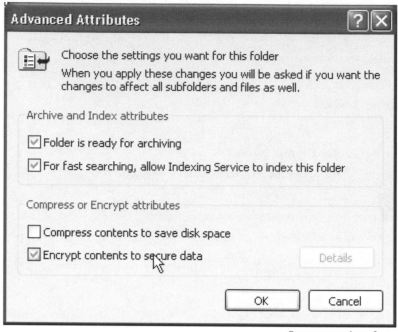

Figure 3-6   Encrypting a file.

How to Encrypt a File

To encrypt a file in Windows, follow these steps (Figure 3-6):

1. Right-click the folder to be encrypted and select **Properties.**
2. Select the **Advanced** button in the **General** tab.
3. The **Advanced Attributes** dialog box pops up.
4. There are two options under **Compress or Encrypt Attributes**:
   - Compress contents to save disk space
   - Encrypt contents to secure data
5. Select **Encrypt contents to secure data.**
6. Click **OK** to close the **Compress or Encrypt Attributes** dialog box.
7. Apply the settings and click OK.

Decryption

File *decryption* is a type of file protection that decodes the data within an encrypted file. Decryption goes hand in hand with encryption, and the tool that was used to encrypt the data will be needed, along with the key, to decrypt the data.

Windows EFS Decryption

For Windows EFS decryption, if the user decrypts a folder and its nested files, nothing is encrypted anymore. If the user decrypts the folder and not its nested files, the nested files stay encrypted, but any new files placed there will not be encrypted.

How to Decrypt a File

Here's how to decrypt a file in Windows:

1. Right-click the file to be decrypted and select **Properties.**

2. Select the **Advanced** button in the **General** tab.

3. The **Advanced Attributes** dialog box pops up.

4. There are two options under **Compress or Encrypt Attributes:**

   - Compress contents to save disk space

   - Encrypt contents to secure data

5. Uncheck **Encrypt contents to secure data.**

6. Click **OK** to close the **Compress or Encrypt Attributes** dialog box.

7. Apply the settings and click OK.

Lock/Unlock the Computer

How do you protect your computer when it is on but you aren't at your desk (maybe you are in a meeting or getting coffee)? Lock/unlock the computer is a built-in feature of Windows Operating system NT/2000/XP for securing the computer from any unauthorized user.

To lock a computer (Figure 3-7):

1. Press the Ctrl+Alt+Delete keys simultaneously.

2. Click the **Lock Computer** button.

To unlock a computer:

1. Press the Ctrl+Alt+Delete keys simultaneously.

2. Enter the legitimate password in the password form.

3. Press Enter.

Employing Screensaver Password

Also remember that a screensaver alone will not prevent people from accessing your desktop, but you can employ a screensaver password to discourage someone from trying.

Follow these steps to employ a screensaver password (Figure 3-8):

1. Right-click the desktop.

2. Click **Properties.**

3. Select the **Screen Saver** tab.

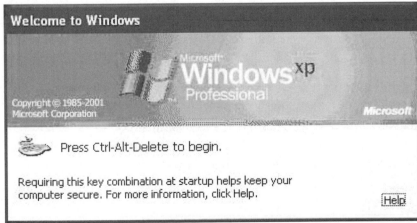

Source: www.microsoft.com

Figure 3-7 Locking the computer.

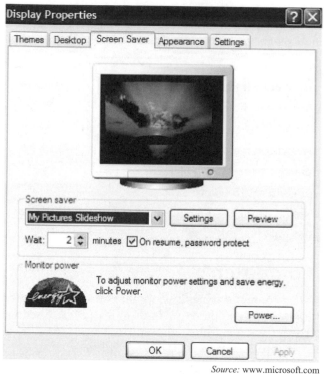

Figure 3-8 Setting a screensaver password.

4. Select a screen saver in the drop-down window.

5. Check the On resume, password protect option and select the waiting time for the idle screen in the Wait box.

6. Apply the settings by clicking the **Apply** button.

7. Press the Ctrl+Alt+Delete keys simultaneously and enter the legitimate password to access the workstation.

Using Task Manager

Do you find that your computer gets slow every now and then? When this slowdown happens, you might find that one of your programs is slow to respond and runs even when you don't want it to. You can use Task Manager to stop the program from using resources when the program is not responding to a close or exit command.

1. Choose one of these ways to open Windows Task Manager.
   - Press the Ctrl+Alt+Delete keys simultaneously and click on the **Task Manager** button.
   - Right-click the **Task Bar.** Click **Task Manager.**
   - Choose **Start -> Run -> taskmgr**
   - Press Ctrl+Shift+Esc simultaneously.

2. Three tabs are presented in the Task Manager: Applications, Processes, Performance.

3. Find out what applications are running by pressing the **Applications** tab.

4. Find out what processes are running by pressing the **Processes** tab (Figure 3-9).

A **process** is a single executable element that runs concurrently with other executable elements.

5. Find out what the CPU usage and memory usage are by pressing the **Performance** tab.

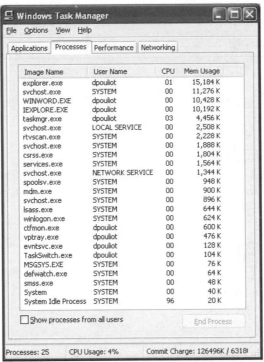

Source: www.microsoft.com

Figure 3-9 The **Processes** tab in Windows Task Manager.

Run/Kill Processes

Suppose that you discover that a program that is not responding is called "expert analyst." You find this information from the task manager. When you press the **Processes** tab, you see a **process** called "eanalyst" taking up 93% of the CPU cycles. You need to stop this process to work productively. What can you do?

To kill a particular process, follow these steps:

1. Select the target process and click the **End Process** button.

2. Select the target process, right-click it, and select **End Process.**

To run a particular process, follow these steps:

- Click File -> New Task (Run). Enter the name of the process to run.

Killing Process Trees

You can kill process trees by following these steps (Figure 3-10):

 A ***process tree*** displays the hierarchy in a tree structure of all the instances of a program being executed. Programs are sets of instructions, and a process is the actual execution of those instructions.

1. Run the Task Manager.

2. Select the target process and click the **End Process** button or right-click it and select **End Process Tree.**

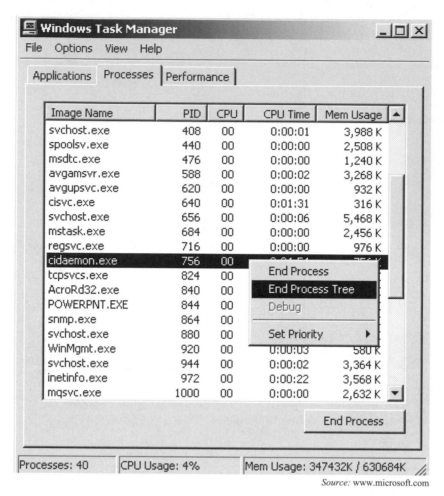

Source: www.microsoft.com

Figure 3-10   Killing Process Trees.

Identifying Suspicious Processes and Applications

Task Manager can also be effective as a precautionary measure to identify unknown applications and processes running on the system without the knowledge or consent of the user. Task Manager has its limits, as some rogue or malicious applications cannot be identified using it.

The Task Manager can also be used to stop unknown processes using the End Process function and unknown applications can be stopped using End Task function in Task Manager. Stealth applications such as keyloggers and dialers cannot be found using Task Manager, and the user may need an antispyware tool to detect and remove stealth applications. A *keylogger* is a program that records the keystrokes made by a user on a computer. *Malicious dialer programs* are a type of spyware that can install itself to your dial-up settings to redirect Internet connections.

Downloading Applications Securely

You should be aware of locations on the Internet where safe programs can be downloaded securely. Downloading programs or applications or files from unknown Web sites or illegal URLs on the Internet may harm your system because there is a chance of infecting the system with a virus, Trojan horse, or malware. Scan the file using effective antivirus software after downloading it (Figure 3-11). Open the file only after the scan results show that the file is not malicious or it is malware free.

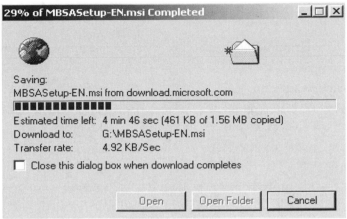

Source: www.microsoft.com

Figure 3-11 Downloading files safely.

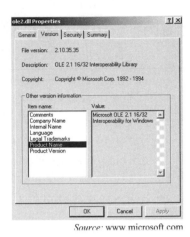

Source: www.microsoft.com

Figure 3-12 Version tab in DLL properties.

Using Checksum

File integrity can be checked using MD5 checksum. File Checksum and Integrity Verifier (FCIV), a command prompt utility can be used to compute cryptographic hash values. Cryptographic hash values are often called (digital) fingerprints. FCIV can be downloaded from *http://www.download.microsoft.com*. Microsoft Windows 2000, Windows XP, and Windows Server 2003 support FCIV. Type in the following command to check the integrity of a suspicious file:

c:\> **fciv.exe suspectfilename**

The hash value of the suspect file will be shown. The user can then cross-check the given output to the already known hash value of the original file for comparison. Some features of the FCIV utility are:

- By default FCIV uses the MD5 hash algorithm but it also supports SHA1.
- The output generated can be stored in an XML file.
- Generates recursive output of hash values for all files in a particular directory, including the subdirectories.
- Supplies an exception list to specify files or directories to hash.
- Ability to store hash values for a file with or without the full path of the file.

Security Aspects of Dynamic Library Linked (DLL) Files

Dynamic Library Linked (DLL) files are used to combine multiple programs to give the appearance that a single program is running. Authenticity of DLL files downloaded from third-party sources cannot be trusted. Most of the third-party sources host the DLL files in *.zip format; therefore, you should follow these steps:

1. Scan the downloaded file with an updated antivirus program to check for malware.
2. Right-click the DLL file and go to **Properties** to check for its authenticity.
3. Click the **Version** tab (Figure 3-12) to find more information about the DLL.
4. The **Version** tab shows the authenticity of the DLL file and the name of the vendor who supplied the DLL file.

Chapter Summary

- Only folders can be shared—not files. Ensure authorized access to shared folders by assigning permissions.
- Files and folders can be hidden from view.
- Use caution when transferring and downloading files.
- Use backup and restore to protect data. File backup is a type of file safeguarding method that enables you to store copies of critical files and folders on another medium for safekeeping.
- Data restoration is a type of information protection scheme that enables the user to recover stored copies of files and folders from another medium.
- Encrypt confidential folders. Encryption protects data by camouflaging it within a file or message, so that unauthorized users cannot use it. File decryption is a type of file protection that decodes the data within an encrypted file.
- Use Task Manager to end unresponsive and suspicious processes.
- The user must be aware of locations on the Internet where safe programs can be downloaded securely. Check hash values of downloaded files to ensure integrity.

Review Questions

1. Pressing the _____ + _____ + _____ keys simultaneously pops up a window to lock the computer.

2. How do you share a folder on a system running Windows XP? Write down all the steps.

   _____

   _____

   _____

   _____

3. How do you hide a folder on a system running Windows XP? Write down all the steps.

   _____

   _____

   _____ _____ _____ _____

   _____

4. _____ can be used to kill unwanted processes.

5. How do you back up a file? Write down all the steps.

   _____

   _____

   _____

   _____

6. How do you encrypt a file stored on a system running Windows XP? Write down all the steps.

   _____

   _____

   _____

   _____

7. The MD5 checksum checks the _____ of the file.

8. FCIV is used to check the _____ of the file.

9. _____ can be used as a precautionary measure that can identify unknown applications cesses running on the system without the knowledge or consent of the user.

10. How do you confirm the authenticity of a DLL file? Write down all the steps.

_____

_____

_____

_____

Hands-On Projects

1. Back up and restore a particular file.

2. Enable a password-protected screensaver to lock your workstation after 10 minutes of idle screen.

3. Enable file sharing with appropriate permissions to another user or group.

4. Look for a suspicious process running on your system and kill it.

Case Example

John, who works as a research officer with an educational institute, was catching up with his work at home. His work was interrupted by a call and he left his system unattended to answer the telephone call.

Ronnie, his eight-year-old, took the opportunity to play on the computer. Unaware of the consequences of his actions, Ronnie closed a few applications to play his favorite game. When John got back from his call, he saw Ronnie busy on his computer. He realized to his horror that he hadn't saved the file he was working on and that the word processor was closed. To add to his worry, John had turned off the autosave option in the word processor.

1. What could John have done to ensure that nobody used his computer while he was away from it?

    a. Shutdown the system.

    b. Log off the system.

    c. Lock the workstation.

    d. Start the screensaver.

2. What can John do to ensure that Ronnie is not able to access important resources?

    a. Create a new user account for Ronnie.

    b. Assign rights to everyone for important files and folders.

    c. Buy Ronnie a new system.

    d. Give Ronnie specific time on the system.

3. How can John keep an important folder away from unauthorized users?

   a. Hide it.

   b. Lock it.

   c. Scramble it.

   d. Put it on a different drive.

4. John wants to share his project folder with his teammate securely. He should ideally

   a. Enable file and print sharing.

   b. Use e-mail.

   c. Use a USB flash disk.

   d. Use Web folders.

5. How can John use a screensaver to protect himself?

   a. Use a matrix screensaver.

   b. Use a password with the screensaver.

   c. Use an encrypted screensaver.

   d. Use a moving screensaver.

Chapter 4

Administering Windows Securely

Objectives

After completing this chapter, you should be able to:

- Use the Event Viewer
- Read logs on your system
- Enable auditing in Windows
- Locate and use the Windows registry
- Restore the registry
- Close ports
- Find services and ports they listen on
- Use common internal commands

Key Terms

Application log   an event log that records information about the performance of software applications

Auditing   a manual or automatic systematic, measurable technical assessment of a system or application

Event logs   events that are reported by the operating system

Event Viewer   a Windows operating system application that graphically displays a log of events

File Transfer Protocol (FTP)   one of the TCP/IP protocols that is used to copy files between two computers on the Internet

Internal commands   these Windows XP commands remain in memory at all times and are available to the user at all times

Key (in registry events)   a key in the registry is similar to a folder in that it contains a subkey and a value entry, it can also be used to carry out functions

Port   a route into and out of a computer or network device

Registry   a system entity that provides service and service-provider information, and configuration data, in a hierarchical structure

Security log   an event log that maintains information about the success or failure of audited events; specifically, it contains information on security events that are specified in the audit policy

System log   a record of events that concern components of the system itself, such as device driver or network failure

TCP/IP   the protocols, or principles, that computers use to communicate over the Internet

Values (in registry)   the string of characters that appear in the right pane of the registry window; it defines the value of the currently selected key

Windows Registry Editor   Registry Editor is used to view and edit the contents of the registry

Case Example

Mary Jane works as a resource developer on the human resources team of a renowned stock brokerage company. She has a computer at her house, which she uses to record her everyday activities and her personal finances. Her computer runs on Windows XP, and she uses Office XP to record her activities. One evening as she was doing her usual work on her home computer, she noticed a change in the system's behavior. So, she scanned her system with an antivirus program, which found some rogue files with .exe extensions. Mary Jane was surprised, because she had scanned her computer earlier in the evening and that scan hadn't found any problems, and she hadn't been surfing the Web.

What should Mary Jane do next to find out what is going on and to protect her computer from attacks?

Introduction

This chapter will introduce some of the built-in features of Windows that can help you work more securely. The chapter concludes with a list of some basic internal commands that can be used for troubleshooting.

Overview of Event Viewer

Follow these steps (in Windows NT, 2000, XP) to locate the Event Viewer:

Start -> Settings -> Control Panel -> Administrative Tools -> Event Viewer

Logs about applications, security, and system events are stored in the *Event Viewer,* which is a Windows operating system application that graphically displays a log of events. You can use these logs to gather information about hardware, software, and system problems. In addition, Event Viewer allows centralized monitoring of events on a network. *Event logs* come in handy while investigating any problems or anomalies in the computer or network because they log events reported by the operating system. With event logs the user can track a problem and diagnose it.

A Windows (NT, 2000, XP, 2003)-based computer records events in the following three logs (Figure 4-1):

- The *Application log* contains events such as errors, warnings, or information logged by applications. Events are classified by type (severity), with "information" at the low end, "warning" in the middle, and "error" at the high end of severity.

- The *Security log* maintains information about the success or failure of audited events. A security policy enables the auditing process, or the monitoring of security-related events, which records them in the security log for review.

- The *System log* includes events generated by system components, such as driver failures and hardware issues.

How to Read Logs on Your System

Go to Event Viewer. Choose the log you wish to review, right-click any of the log entries in the window, and select **Properties** to learn about the event in detail. The Event Viewer shows all the events in a table. Each event log is differentiated by its type and contains header information and a description of the event (Figure 4-2).

Each event header contains a detailed description of the following:

- *Type*: Event Viewer categorizes events into five types: Error, Warning, Information, Success Audit, or Failure Audit. This entry shows the type of event that occurred.

- *Date*: The system date on which the event occurred.

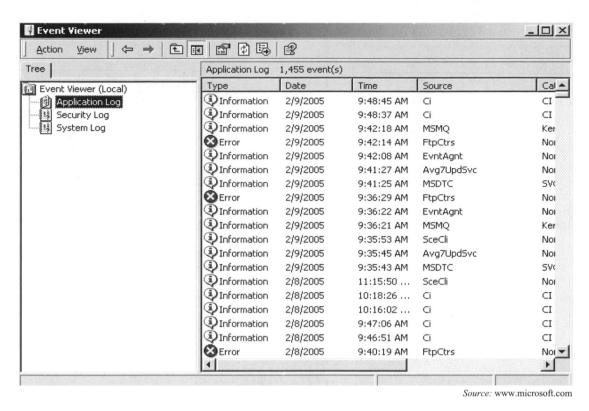

Source: www.microsoft.com

Figure 4-1   Event Viewer.

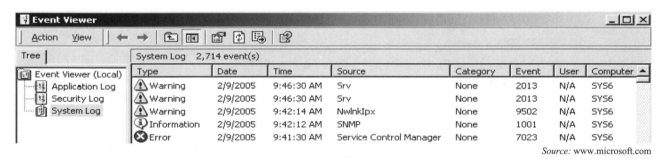

Source: www.microsoft.com

Figure 4-2   Reading logs.

- *Time*: The system time at which the event occurred.
- *Source*: The source of the event.
- *Category*: Classification of the event by the event source.
- *Event ID*: Event is the ID number of a particular event that identifies the source.
- *User*: Username of the user who logged on at the time of the event.
- *Computer*: Name of the computer where the event occurred.

How to Enable Auditing on Your System

The security log maintains information about the success or failure of audited events. A security policy enables the *auditing* process, which records them in the security log for review. Auditing is a manual or automatic systematic, measurable technical assessment of a system or application. You must turn this feature on, and determine which events should be monitored and recorded in the security log.

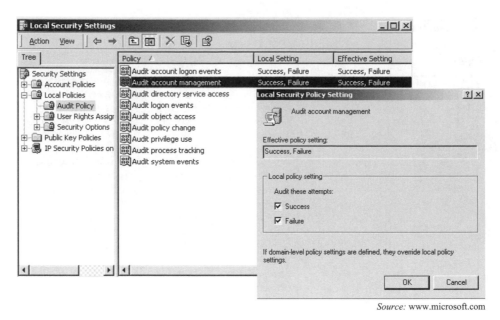

Source: www.microsoft.com

Figure 4-3   Enabling auditing.

Log on to Windows with administrative rights, and follow these steps (depending on the version of your operating system, the steps may vary slightly) (Figure 4-3):

1. Click on the **Start** button of the Windows operating system.

2. Click on **Settings**.

3. From Settings, go to Control Panel.

4. Double-click on **Administrative Tools** on the Control Panel.

5. Open **Local Security Policy** in the Administrative Tools.

6. Open **Local Policies**.

7. Drop down the **Local Policies** and click **Audit Policy**.

8. In the **Audit Policy** window, right-click on any one of the events and click **Security** to open **Local Security Policy Setting**. Mark the type of events to be logged.

Audit events can be split into two categories: (1) Success events: A success event indicates successful access gained by the user; and (2) Failure events: A failure event indicates an unsuccessful attempt made to gain the access to a resource.

A word of caution. These logs can become very large. Be sure to choose properties of each log file so you know where it is located and choose how you want to control the file size.

Overview of Windows Registry

Configuration information for the Windows operating system is stored in a database called the *registry*. User profiles, information related to system hardware, programs installed on the system, and property settings are stored in the registry. There is a built-in tool in Windows called the ***Windows Registry Editor***, used to view and edit the registry.

Two versions of Registry Editor exist in Windows 2000: (1) Regedt32.exe (32-bit), installed in the systemroot\system32 folder; and (2) Regedit.exe (16-bit), installed in the systemroot folder.

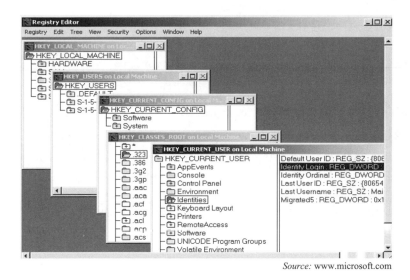

Source: www.microsoft.com

Figure 4-4 Opening Regedt32.exe.

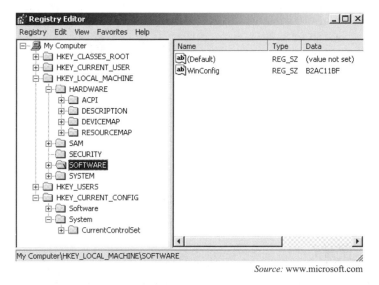

Source: www.microsoft.com

Figure 4-5 Opening Regedit.exe.

Opening Regedt32.exe

Follow these steps to start Regedt32.exe (Figure 4-4):

1. Go to **Start**.
2. Type **Run**.
3. Type **regedt32**.
4. Click **OK**.

Opening Regedit.exe

Follow these steps to start Regedit.exe (Figure 4-5):

1. Go to **Start**.
2. Type **Run**.
3. Type **regedit**.
4. Click **OK**.

Understanding Registry Entries

As Figure 4-6 shows, the left pane of the Windows Registry Editor is the tree view with folders named *keys*. The right pane of the Windows Registry Editor shows contents of the selected keys. Each key can have subkeys. The contents are called values.

Values are the string of characters that appear in the right pane of the registry window. It defines the value of the currently selected key and the three types are:

1. String (REG_SZ: A fixed-length text string.)

2. Binary (REG_BINARY: Raw binary data. Most hardware component information is stored as binary data and is displayed in Registry Editor in hexadecimal format.)

3. DWORD (REG_DWORD: Data represented by a number that is 4 bytes long [a 32-bit integer]. Many parameters for device drivers and services are this type and are displayed in Registry Editor in binary, hexadecimal, or decimal format.)

Restoring Registry Settings

System registry settings can be changed using the Windows Registry Editor. Be careful, though. If the registry settings are altered incorrectly, then there is a high risk that the computer may not function properly; however, you can restore registry settings.

To restore the registry settings:

1. Go to **Start**.

2. Click **Shutdown** button.

3. Click **Restart**.

4. Click **OK**.

During the restart of the OS the message, "Please select the operating system to start," will be shown on the screen; press F8. Turn off the Num Lock on the keyboard. Use the arrow keys to select the option "Last Known Good Configuration" and hit Enter. Use the arrow keys again to select the OS and hit Enter. The Last Known Good Configuration is a saved copy of all the registry settings that the system knows will perform a successful boot, and may restore device drivers if you recently replaced them. Problems related to corrupted or missing files or drivers cannot be rectified by the above method.

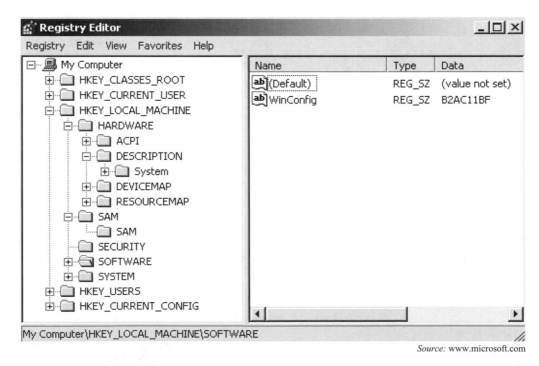

Source: www.microsoft.com

Figure 4-6   Registry entries.

How to Close a Port

A *port* is a route into and out of a computer or network device. It is important to close ports for services that are not needed by the user. Attackers target open ports of specific services. For example, a person who uses the computer just for chatting and sending e-mails need not have port 21 open. Port 21 is for *FTP* (File Transfer Protocol), which is one of the TCP/IP protocols that is used to copy files between two computers on the Internet. *TCP/IP* is the set of communications protocols used for the Internet. Most operating systems now include and install the TCP/IP stack by default. It uses encapsulation and layers to provide services. Ports, such as 21 for FTP, are in the top layer. It is supported by TCP, which in turn is supported by IP. The name of the protocol suite is made of the two most significant parts, TCP and IP. One of the following steps can be used to close ports that are not necessary for the user (Figure 4-7):

1. Login as administrator.

2. **Start -> Settings -> Control Panel -> Administrative Tools -> Services.**

3. Right-click on any of the unnecessary services and click **Stop**.

Follow these steps to block TCP/UDP ports (Figure 4-8):

1. Go to **Control Panel**.

2. Select **Network and Dial-up Connections.**

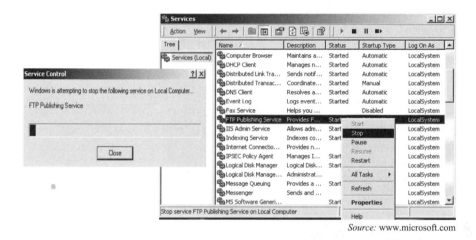

Source: www.microsoft.com

Figure 4-7   Closing port 21.

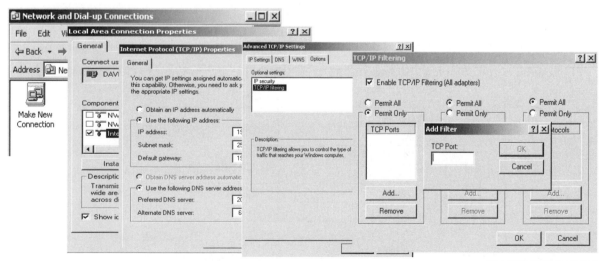

Source: www.microsoft.com

Figure 4-8   Blocking TCP/UDP ports.

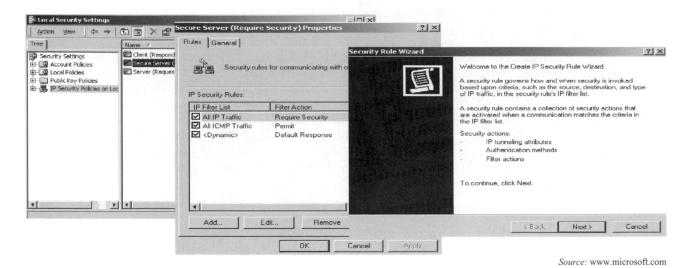

Figure 4-9   Applying security policies to a port.

3. Open **Local Area Connection**.

4. Right-click and select **Properties** from the menu.

5. Select **Internet Protocol (TCP/IP)** and click the **Properties** button.

6. Click **Advanced** and then select **Options**.

7. Select **TCP/IP Filtering** and then **Properties**.

8. Here you will determine what to allow or deny.

Follow these steps to apply security policies to closing a port (Figure 4-9):

1. Go to **Control Panel**.

2. Double-click on **Administrative Tools**.

3. Select **Local Security Policy**.

4. Select **IP Security Policies on Local Computer**.

5. Open **Secure Server**.

6. Finally click **Add**.

Services and the Ports They Listen On

Following is a list of a few services and ports on which they listen (Figure 4-10):

netstat	15
ftp	21
Telnet	23
SMTP	25
DNS	53
www-http	80
POP3	110
NetBIOS	139
SNMP	161
IRC	531

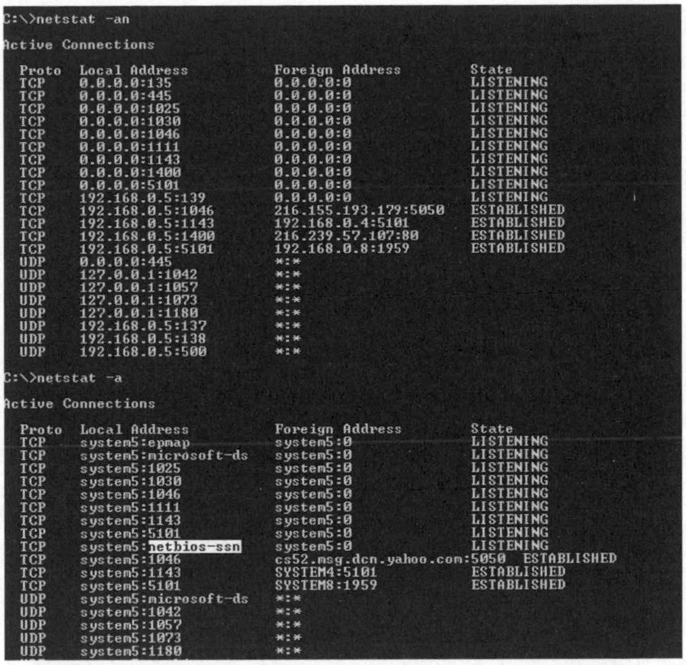

Source: www.microsoft.com

Figure 4-10   Services and their ports.

OS Internal Commands for Basic Operations

Internal commands are available within the default command interpreter (cmd.exe) in Windows XP. They are used in scripts because they do not require disk access to load their code. These commands remain in memory at all times and are available to the user at all times.

The syntax for local execution of an internal command is:

- COMMAND [/switches][parameters]
- CALL COMMAND [/switches][parameters]
- cmd.exe /c COMMAND [/switches][parameters]
- %compsec% /c COMMAND [/switches][parameters]

The syntax for remote execution is:

\\computername\admin$\system32\cmd.exe/c COMMAND [/switches][parameters]

The following table shows some of the basic internal commands that a user might find useful when troubleshooting.

Command	Description	Examples	Parameters
arp	Displays and modifies the IP-to-Ethernet or token ring physical address translation tables used by the Address Resolution Protocol (ARP).	**arp** parameter [*inet_addr*] [**-N** [*if_addr*]] **arp** parameter inet_addr [if_addr] **arp** parameter inet_addr ether_addr [if_addr]]	
netstat	Displays protocol statistics and current TCP/IP network connections.	**netstat** [**-a**] [**-e**] [**-n**] [**-s**] [**-p** *protocol*] [**-r**] [*interval*]	
finger	Displays information about a user on a specified system running the Finger service. Output will differ based on the remote system.	**finger** [**-l**] [*user*]\@ *computer* [. . .]	
ipconfig	Displays all current TCP/IP network configuration values.	**ipconfig** [**/all** | **/renew** [*adapter*] **/release** [*adapter*]]	**all** Produces a full display. Without this switch, ipconfig displays only the IP address, subnet mask, and default gateway values for each network card. **/renew** [*adapter*] Renews DHCP configuration parameters. **/release** [*adapter*] Releases the current DHCP configuration. With no parameters, the ipconfig utility presents all of the current TCP/IP configuration values to the user, including IP address and subnet mask. This utility is especially useful on systems running DHCP, allowing users to determine which values have been configured by DHCP.
nbtstat	Displays protocol statistics and current TCP/IP connections using NBT (NetBIOS over TCP/IP).	**nbtstat** [**-a** *remotename*] [**-A** *IP address*] [**-c**] [**-n**] [**-R**] [**-r**] [**-S**] [**-s**] [*interval*]	**-a** *remotename* Lists the remote computer's name table using its name. **-A** *IP address* Lists the remote computer's name table using its IP address. **-c** Lists the contents of the NetBIOS name cache giving the IP address of each name. **-n** Lists local NetBIOS names. **-R** Reloads the Lmhosts file after purging all names from the NetBIOS name cache. **-r** Lists name resolution statistics for Windows networking name resolution. **-S** Displays both client and server sessions, listing the remote computers by IP address only. **-s** Lists the NetBIOS sessions table converting destination IP addresses to computer NetBIOS names.

Table 4-1   Basic internal commands for troubleshooting

(continues)

Command	Description	Examples	Parameters
nslookup	Displays information from domain name system (DNS) name servers. Before using this tool, you should be familiar with how DNS works.		-option... Specifies one or more nslookup commands as a command-line option. The command line length must be less than 256 characters. computer-to-find Looks up information for computer-to-find using the current default server or using server, if specified. server Specifies to use this server as the DNS name server. If you omit server, the default DNS name server is used.
ping	Verifies connections to a remote computer or computers.	**ping** [-t] [-a] [-n count] [-l length] [-f] [-i ttl] [-v tos] [-r count] [-s count] [[-j computer-list] | [-k computer-list]] [-w timeout] destination-list	-t Pings the specified computer until interrupted. -a Resolves addresses to computer names. -n count Sends the number of ECHO packets specified by count. The default is 4. -l length Sends ECHO packets containing the amount of data specified by length. The default is 32 bytes; the maximum is 65,527. -f Sends a Do not Fragment flag in the packet. The packet will not be fragmented by gateways on the route. -i ttl Sets the Time To Live field to the value specified by ttl. -v tos Sets the Type Of Service field to the value specified by tos. -r count Records the route of the outgoing packet and the returning packet in the Record Route field. A minimum of 1 and a maximum of 9 computers can be specified by count. -s count Specifies the time stamp for the number of hops specified by count. -j computer-list Routes packets by way of the list of computers specified by computer-list. Consecutive computers can be separated by intermediate gateways (loose source routed). The maximum number allowed by IP is 9. -k computer-list Routes packets by way of the list of computers specified by computer-list. -w timeout Specifies a time-out interval in milliseconds. destination-list Specifies the remote computers to ping.

Table 4-1 Basic internal commands for troubleshooting

(continues)

Command	Description	Examples	Parameters
echo	Turns the command-echoing feature on or off, or displays a message.	**echo** [**on**	**off**] [*message*]	**on**	**off** Specifies whether to turn the command-echoing feature on or off. To display the current **echo** setting, use the echo command without a parameter. *message* Specifies text you want Windows 2000 to display on the screen.
netconfig	Displays the configurable services that are running, or displays and changes settings for a service.	**net config** [*service* [*options*]]	none Type **net config** without parameters to display a list of configurable services. *service* Specifies a service (server or workstation) that can be configured with the **net config** command.

Table 4-1 Basic internal commands for troubleshooting *continued*

Chapter Summary

- Events related to hardware, software, and system components can be viewed using Event Viewer.
- Event Viewer can view centralized monitoring of events on a network.
- Each event log is differentiated by its type and contains header information and a description of the event.
- A success event indicates successful access gained by the user, as an example; whereas a failure event indicates an unsuccessful attempt to gain the access to a resource.
- Configuration information for the Windows operating system is stored in a database called the registry.
- The left pane of the Windows Registry Editor is the tree view with folders called *keys*.
- System registry settings can be changed using the Windows Registry Editor.
- It is important to close ports for services that are not needed by the user. Attackers target open ports of specific services.
- Internal commands are available within the default command interpreter (cmd.exe) in Windows XP.

Review Questions

1. What are the three types of event logs stored in Event Viewer?

   _____

   _____

   _____

   _____

2. The Registry is a database that stores _____ information for the Windows OS.

3. What are the two versions of Registry Editor in Windows 2000?

   _____

   _____

   _____

   _____

4. The contents of the left pane of the Windows Registry Editor are called _____.

5. What service runs on port 21?

_____

_____

_____

_____

6. The _____ command displays all current TCP/IP network configuration values, when executed.

7. What feature can you use in Windows to keep tabs on who has logged on or off a system?

_____

_____

_____

_____

8. The _____ maintains information about the success or failure of audited events.

9. The _____ contains the events, such as errors, warnings, or information, logged by applications.

10. The _____ includes events generated by system components.

11. What are the three types of values in a registry?

_____

_____

_____

_____

12. The _____ command displays protocol statistics and current TCP/IP network connections.

13. The _____ command displays protocol statistics and current TCP/IP connections using NBT (NetBIOS over TCP/IP)

Hands-On Projects

HANDS-ON PROJECTS

1. Close the FTP port (be sure to reopen it if you need to use that service).

2. Read the system logs to find problems or anomalies in the system.

3. Find statistics about your computer using the netstat command and switches.

4. Find the IP address of the system.

5. Use the ping command to check for connectivity.

Chapter 5

Security Threats and Attacks

Objectives

After completing this chapter, you should be able to:

- Recognize the various security threats and attacks, including:
  - Social engineering
  - Phishing
  - Viruses
  - Trojans
  - Worms
  - Spyware
  - Adware
  - Keyloggers
  - Denial of service
  - Spamming
  - Port Scanners
  - Password crackers

Key Terms

Adware   type of spyware that gathers information about the user in order to exhibit advertisements in the Web browser based on the classification made from the user's browsing patterns

Denial-of-service attack (DoS)   an attack on a computer system or network that causes a loss of service to users

Dictionary attack   attack that tries passwords and/or keys from a compiled list of common words or passwords

Distributed denial of service (DDoS)   form of an attack in which the attacking computer hosts are often computers with broadband connections that have been compromised, unknown to the user, by viruses or Trojan horse programs that allow the attacker to remotely control the machines and direct the attack

Phishing   the illegal acquisition of sensitive personal information, such as passwords and credit card details, by criminals pretending to be legitimate entities with a real need for such information

Port scanner   verifies which ports are open on an IP address and reads any data sent when it connects

Port scanning   program that tries to find the weaknesses of a computer or network device by frequently inquiring it with requests for information

Shareware   copyrighted commercial software that is distributed without payment on a trial basis and is limited by any combination of functionality, availability, or convenience

Social engineering   the practice of conning people into revealing sensitive data on a computer system or information that can be used on networks and systems

Spam   unsolicited commercial e-mail

Spamming   the practice of mailing out spam

Spyware   a type of malicious software that gathers and reports information about a computer user without the user's knowledge or consent

Case Example

John recently installed the Lycos antispam screensaver that he received in an e-mail attachment titled, "Lycos screensaver to fight spam.zip." According to the e-mail, Lycos had recently announced the screensaver as a means to combat spammers.

Alice downloaded a software package, ShareIT 3.1 that will allow her to share files over the Internet using a peer-to-peer sharing site. Unbeknownst to Alice, the company has "bundled" a "great value" application, StealthDialer.exe, which is a hidden dialer application.

When Alice opens her Web browser after installation of the software package, the dialer opens in a hidden window and dials a phone number without her knowledge. Alice cannot figure out why she is being served unsolicited content by her browser.

She finds her home page reset and cannot find a way to uninstall this downloaded program, and her phone bill is higher than normal.

Denise always clicks **OK** whenever she is prompted to by her computer. All she wants is to continue browsing without being asked too many questions. She likes that "useful" software that helps her enter information on Web pages automatically.

Before long, she finds it strange that advertisements are being displayed on her screen—and even stranger that they are related to her recent Web searches.

What risks are John, Alice, and Denise taking in their computer-using habits? Can you identify what has occurred in each situation? If you were advising them, what would you tell them to do in the above scenarios?

Introduction

This chapter introduces the various security threats and attacks to which today's computer user is vulnerable. We define security threats, attacks, and vulnerabilities as follows:

- A *security threat* is a potential danger to the safety of data and software on a personal computer (PC).
- A *security attack* is said to have occurred when the security of data or software on a PC is compromised.
- A *security vulnerability* is a flaw in a product that poses a threat and exposes the system to an attack, even in intended use.

Social Engineering

Social engineering is the practice of conning people into revealing sensitive data on a computer system or information that can be used on networks and systems. It can be a simple telephone call from someone claiming to be with the ISP (Internet service provider), asking for details to reset the account or it can be an elaborate e-mail hoax (phishing).

Many users, however, will unwisely click on any attachments they receive, thus allowing the attack to succeed. A contemporary example of a social engineering attack is the use of e-mail attachments that contain malicious payloads that, for instance, use the victim's machine to send massive quantities of spam to other victims.

Internet users frequently receive messages that request password or credit card information in order to "set up an account" or "reactivate settings."

Other examples of social engineering include:

- Con e-mails (free vacation)
- Pop-ups (sweepstakes win or nth visitor prize or a free membership—Figure 5-1)
- Phone calls or survey visits asking for information
- Peeping over shoulders
- Checking dumpsters for information

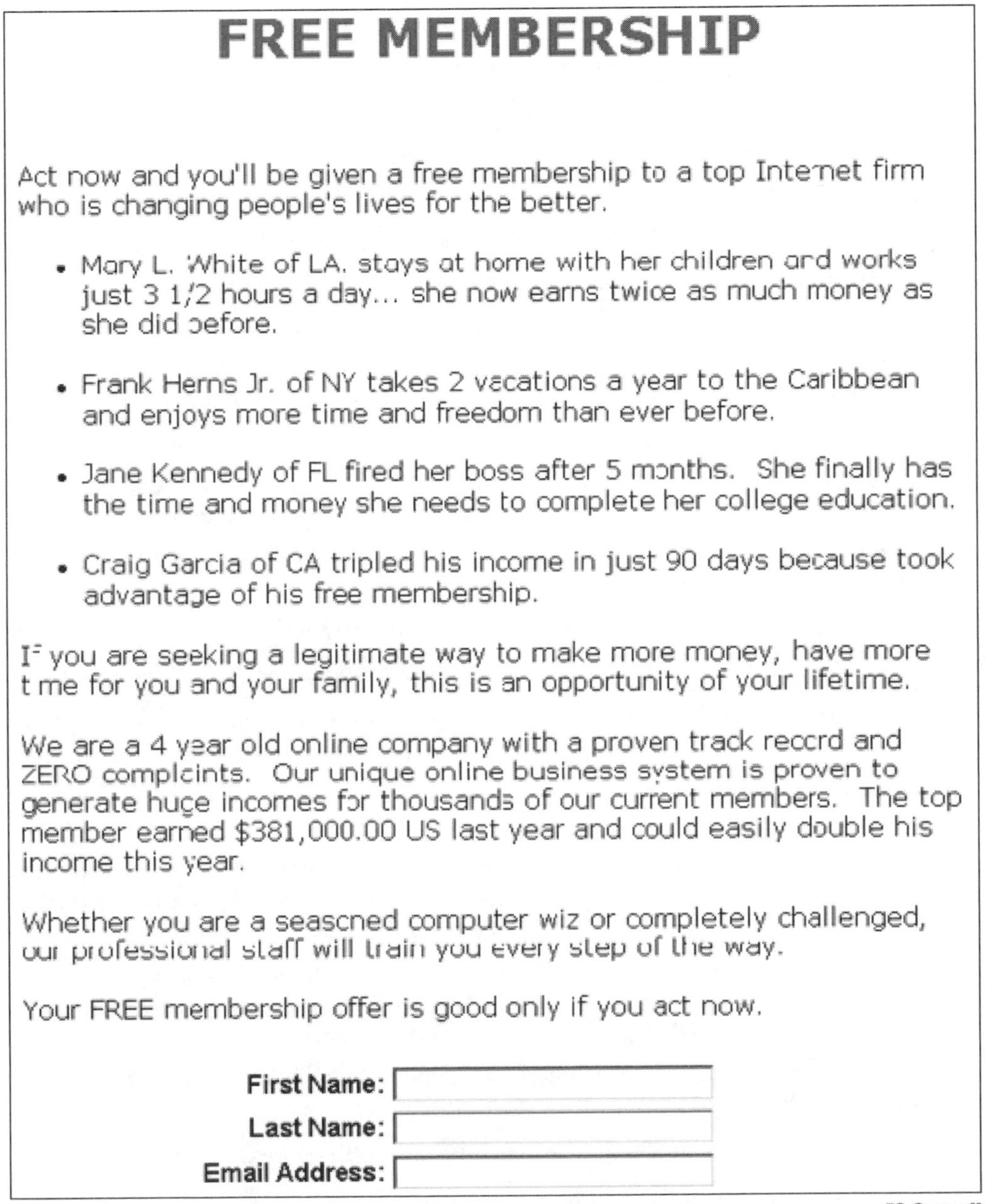

Figure 5-1 Social engineering is a nontechnical nature of intrusion that relies heavily on human interaction and often involves tricking other people to break normal security procedures. This "offer" is an example.

Phishing

Phishing is the illegal acquisition of sensitive personal information, such as passwords and credit card details, by criminals pretending to be legitimate entities with a real need for such information. The term *phishing* is shorthand for *password harvesting fishing*.

Online criminals use phishing because it is profitable. Popular lure Web sites are online banking services and auction sites. Phishers send out spam e-mails to a large number of potential victims that trick the recipients into visiting a Web page that appears to be legitimate. The goal of the phisher is to trick the victim into divulging personal information.

As mentioned previously, a phishing e-mail will appear to come from a trustworthy company (e.g., Amazon, PayPal, eBay) and contain a subject and message intended to con the recipient into taking action. A common ploy is to tell recipients that their accounts have been deactivated due to a problem and ask them to take action to reactivate them. The victims are provided with a convenient link in the same e-mail that takes them to a fake Web page. If the user enters personal information on the fake Web page, it is then captured by the attacker and can be used to steal money or the victim's identity.

Here are several ways of faking Web site addresses in e-mails or links used by phishers:

- Using an IP address, e.g., *http://10.10.0.5/*, instead of a URL

  This strategy works if the user ignores the URL bar completely or is confused by the IP address listing.

- Using a completely different domain name, e.g., *https://www.evildomain.com/*

  This ploy works if the user does not pay attention to the domain name at all.

- Using an authentic-sounding but fake domain name, e.g., *https://www.paypal-secure.com*

  This trick works if the user is unfamiliar with the correct domain name.

- Using a subtle letter or number substitution, e.g., *https://www.paypa1.com* (where the number "1" is used instead of the letter "L")

  This technique works if the user does not notice the similar letter/number substitution.

- Using an invisible letter substitution (punycode attack), e.g., *https://www.xn--pypal-4ve.com*

  This discrepancy in the URL may not be seen unless the link is pasted into a text editor like Notepad. Punycode is a method to translate unrecognized international characters.

- Using an address with a username that looks like a domain name, e.g., *http://www.amazon.com@ www.evil.com*

The goal of this strategy is that the victim will be fooled into thinking the fake username is the domain.

You can protect yourself from phishing by taking these precautions:

- Do not reply or click on the link in an e-mail or pop-up message that asks for personal or financial information. Legitimate companies do not ask for this information via e-mail.

- Do not e-mail personal or financial information. E-mail is not a secure method of transmitting personal information.

- Review credit card and bank account statements as soon as you receive them to determine whether they include any unauthorized charges. If your statement is late or missing, call your credit card company or bank to confirm your billing address and account balances.

- Use antivirus software and keep it up to date. Some phishing e-mails contain malicious software (that we will discuss in the following sections) that can harm your system or track your activities on the Internet without your knowledge.

- Be cautious about opening any attachment or downloading any files from e-mails you receive, no matter who they appear to be from.

You should also follow these best practices when you are using e-mail or browsing the Internet:

- Check for the secure site padlock sign.
- Right-click suspicious links and copy and paste them into Notepad to look for subtle changes.
- Read e-mail as a plain text to identify suspicious links.
- Require server verification (https:) for all sites asking critical information.
- Do not click any hyperlinks that you do not trust. Type them in the address bar yourself.

Viruses

As we learned in Chapter 1, viruses are malicious code written with the intention of damaging the victim's computer. They use up system resources and can cause harm by deleting data and critical files, and they can corrupt normal software function.

Why do you need to be aware of the danger viruses pose? There are about 53,000 computer viruses in existence, with a new one detected every 18 seconds. If your system gets infected with a computer virus, it can waste resources and time, and damage your information resources. When you are on the Internet, you are connected to a network, so any virus on your computer can spread to other computers, causing damage to them, as well.

The "ILOVEYOU" virus infected up to 45 million computers and caused more than $5 billion worth of damage worldwide. A computer virus can do anything from displaying a short message to wiping key files so your computer doesn't work. Some viruses may cause direct damage to your files—deleting or corrupting them. Viruses can also use system resources, which will slow down the speed the computer works at by affecting the computer or network. Some viruses can allow others to access and, in some cases, control your computer.

Viruses can spread to your PC via removable media (e.g., floppy disks, CDs, or USB flashdrives) that have been used in other computers. They can also be spread over the network, and also on files that have been attached to e-mails (Figure 5-2). There is usually an infection phase where the virus will spread to as many machines as possible. This spreading of the virus may in itself generate problems, as it could slow down networks and computers by using up their resources. It may then lie dormant until a given time or event when an attack phase might take place. This attack could be to damage files or to make the system slow down.

Trojan Horses

A Trojan horse is a program that looks innocent and useful but is malicious or has harmful code inside. It appears to the user as an apparently harmless program or data, but it creates a backdoor to the machine that the attacker can use to access information assets or system resources unbeknownst to the user. It can damage or erase information on the hard drive. It can also open a discreet means of entry for the attacker to revisit the system and "own" it. The executables usually do not show up in a computer search because they are transparent. The Trojan horse can thus permit an attacker to use the victim's system for further attacks. Data can be stolen and manipulated, or the attacker may use the system's resources, such as hard disk space, to distribute illegal material over the Net.

Some of the other damage a Trojan horse can do include:

- Spreading other malware, such as viruses
- Setting up networks of infected computers in order to attack others
- Retrieving data discreetly from the target computer
- Logging keystrokes to steal information

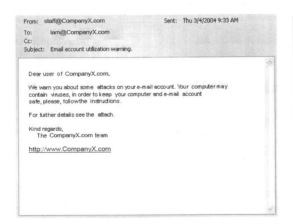

Figure 5-2 Examples of e-mails that entice users to take actions that will infect their computers.

Worms

A computer worm is similar to a computer virus. However, unlike a virus, it does not require user intervention to replicate because it is a self-replicating computer program. A virus works by attaching itself to another executable program. A worm need not be part of another program to propagate itself and is designed to exploit the file transfer activities on target systems.

In addition to replication, the worm can cause further harm such as deleting files on the victim's system or sending documents via e-mail. A worm can wreak havoc on the network due to the amount of traffic it generates by its reproduction. For example, the Mydoom worm caused a noticeable worldwide Internet slowdown at its peak.

More recent worms (e.g., Sobig and Doomjuice) carry other executables (such as packet sniffing software) and allow multiple infections by creating a backdoor for attackers to enter the system again. They turned victim systems into machines used for further attacks. Sometimes such compromised computers are used by spam senders for sending junk e-mail or to hide their Web sites' addresses. The backdoors can also be exploited by other worms, such as Doomjuice, which spreads using the backdoor opened by Mydoom. Nachi was an exception in that it was a worm that tried to find vulnerable Windows machines and install patches to patch the vulnerability. Still it was a nuisance because it rebooted systems without the user's consent.

Following are some interesting variations of viruses and worms:

- Time Bomb—A virus or worm designed to activate at a certain date/time

- Logic Bomb—A virus or worm designed to activate under certain conditions

- Rabbit—A worm designed to replicate to the point of exhausting computer resources

- Bacterium—A virus designed to attach itself to the OS in particular (rather than any application in general) and exhaust computer resources, especially CPU cycles

Spyware

Spyware is a type of malicious software that gathers and reports information about a computer user without the user's knowledge or consent. Spyware can lead to the delivery of undesired advertising (pop-up ads, in particular), rerouting of page requests to illegally claim commercial site referral fees, and even installation of stealth phone dialers, which are malware that can use your modem to dial phone numbers without your knowledge.

Some software providers bundle secondary programs to collect data or distribute advertisements without explicitly informing the user about the real purpose of those programs. These secondary software programs can drastically impair system performance and consume network resources. They often have design features that make them difficult or impossible to uninstall from the system.

Unsecured Windows-based computers, mainly those used by children or inexperienced adults, can swiftly accumulate a great many spyware components. Stealth dialers try to connect directly to a particular telephone number, leading to long-distance or overseas telephone charges. A few spyware vendors, notably 180 Solutions, redirect affiliate links to major online merchants such as eBay and Dell, effectively hijacking the commissions that the affiliates would have expected to earn in the process. Examples of spyware include DirectRevenue, Bonzi Buddy, and Cydoor.

Adware

Adware, or *ad*vertising-supported soft*ware*, is a type of malware that gathers information about the user in order to exhibit advertisements in the Web browser based on classifications made from the user's browsing patterns. These applications include additional code that displays the ads in pop-up windows or through a bar that appears on a computer screen.

Users should also be careful when downloading and installing shareware because some shareware is also adware and is primarily supported by advertising. *Shareware* is copyrighted commercial software offered as a trial version, usually limited in functionality, allowing the user to try it before buying the full version. Paying for a licensed version typically does away with the advertisements (e.g., Download Accelerator). Other types of shareware include demoware, nagware, crippleware, freeware, and spyware.

Figure 5-3 Keystroke logger
attached to a keyboard cable.

A number of software applications are available to help computer users search for and modify adware programs to block the presentation of advertisements and to remove spyware modules.

Keystroke Logging

Keystroke logging is a tool that captures the user's keystrokes. It can be used by an attacker to capture confidential information and use it later. Keyloggers can be both software- and hardware-based. They can be used to find out everything a person types into the computer, including personal letters, business correspondence, passwords, and credit card numbers.

Commercially available keylogging systems include devices that can be attached to the keyboard cable (and thus are instantly installable but visible if the user makes a thorough inspection) and also devices that can be installed in keyboards (and are thus invisible but require some basic knowledge of soldering to install). Software keyloggers, like any computer program, can be distributed as a Trojan horse or as part of a virus or worm. Figure 5-3 shows a keystroke logger attached to a computer's keyboard cable.

Denial of Service

A *denial-of-service attack* (DoS attack) is an attack on a computer system or network that causes a loss of service to users. In this type of attack, legitimate users typically face loss of network connectivity and services because the attack is consuming the bandwidth of the victim network or overloading the computational resources of the victim system. In a *distributed denial-of-service (DDoS)* attack, the attacking computer hosts are often computers with broadband connections that have been compromised, unknown to the user, by viruses or Trojan horse programs that allow the attacker to remotely control the machines and direct the attack. With enough such victims, the services of even the largest and most well-connected Web sites can be denied.

Denial of service can take place because large packets (units of data) are sent or too many packets are sent in a short span of time.

Spamming

Do you receive lots of junk e-mail messages from people you do not know? E-mail has evolved as a much-sought-after tool by marketers to pitch their products and services. Sending bulk messages to recipients who have not solicited them is known as *spamming* and the messages are known as *spam*. E-mail spam is a legitimate cause of concern these days as e-mails can be used for social engineering and phishing attacks, and attachments in unsolicited e-mails can carry viruses or Trojans.

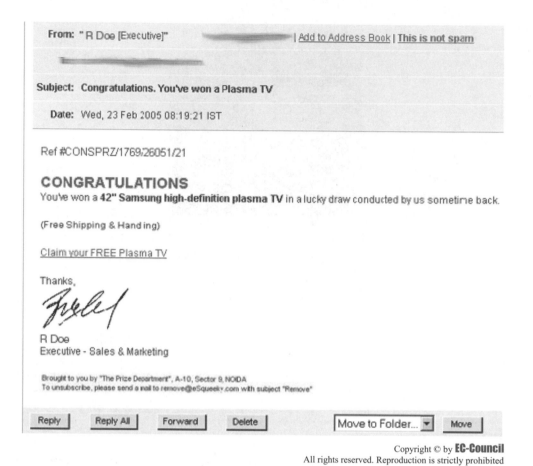

Figure 5-4   Example of spam.

Spamming involves sending identical or nearly identical messages to a large number of recipients. Unlike legitimate commercial e-mail, spam is sent without the explicit permission of the recipients and can bypass e-mail filters using various tricks. Figure 5-4 shows an example of a spam e-mail.

Spammers obtain e-mail addresses by various methods, including harvesting addresses from Web pages; guessing common names at known domains (example: john@microsoft.com). E-pending is the practice of mining data on the Web to match up e-mail addresses with other information about the individual. It is unreliable and can match erroneous records, thereby sending confidential data about one person to someone else.

Most spammers are engaged in illicit activities, such as the porn and gambling industries, and con activities like the Nigerian scammers. Spammers have also created various e-mail viruses that can either use the target for further spamming or for eliciting confidential information. It pays to be aware of where you share your e-mail address.

Port Scanning

A port is a place where information goes into and out of a computer; *port scanning* identifies open doors to a computer. It is a program that tries to find the weaknesses of a computer or network device by frequently inquiring it with requests for information.

Attackers zero in on target computer systems by trying to find out what services run on the system. They can use a port scanner, which will detect open and listening ports on the scanned machine. This information lets them know what applications or programs are used by the target victim. They can then exploit a known or unknown vulnerability to break into the target machine.

A *port scanner* verifies which ports are open on an IP address and reads any data sent when it connects. This application that can let attackers probe a system remotely and target it for an attack based on the information obtained. For example, it can identify the operating system, which attackers can then exploit by using the latest vulnerabilities. It can also take advantage of programs that have known flaws. Regular patch management and closing unused services can help defend against remote scans, and a good firewall will prevent the system from sending information to attackers.

Password Cracking

A password cracker is an application program that is used to identify an unknown or forgotten password to a computer or network resources. Password cracking is the process of recovering secret passwords stored in a computer system. The malicious intent behind password cracking is to gain unauthorized access to a system.

A *dictionary attack* also exploits the tendency of people to choose weak passwords; in this type of attack the intruder tries passwords and/or keys from a compiled list. Password cracking programs usually come equipped with "dictionaries," or word lists, of several kinds. Examples include mythological names, musical artists, places, and commonly used passwords.

A brute force attack tries every possible password. This type of attack is likely to succeed when the password is too short. There are several password cracking programs available on the Internet that intruders can use. A strong password and frequent changes can help defend against password crackers.

Basic Security Measures

You can greatly reduce your vulnerability to these threats and attacks by following some basic security measures:

- Use locks where possible to lock your information assets. Use strong passwords.
- If you are working in an office, make sure that you face the entrance of your office or cubicle and that your screen is not visible to strangers.
- Always ask for identification when someone asks you for personal information.
- Do not trust e-mails, pop-ups, or contest forms from dubious or unknown sources.
- Be careful when you download shareware or freeware. Scan it and check for authenticity of software. You can always do an Internet search for the name or look for it in Wikipedia.
- Read license agreements for software carefully.
- Check Web site privacy policies.
- Verify Web site security by manually checking for the padlock sign and typing the address in the address bar. Never paste or click a link.
- Never hesitate to call up your vendor or a company asking for verification if you suspect information is being gathered for illegal purposes.
- Report spam.

Chapter Summary

- Computer users need to know the basic security threats and attacks that can arise while connected to the Internet.
- Social engineering is an unassuming way of gathering critical information that can be used to compromise an information resource.
- Phishing is the illegal acquisition of sensitive personal information. The victims of phishing can lose money and have their identities stolen.
- Malicious code such as viruses, worms, Trojans, spyware, adware, and keyloggers can harm information resources and compromise the privacy of the user.
- Denial-of-service attacks, spam, and port scanning are all methods that can be used to compromise a system.
- Password crackers can recover and break passwords. They can use a dictionary or a brute force attack.

Review Questions

1. A/An _____ is a program that looks innocent and useful but is malicious or has harmful code inside.

2. A/An _____ does not require user intervention to replicate, as it is a self-replicating computer program.

3. A/An _____ is a virus or worm designed to activate at a certain date/time.

4. A/An _____ is a virus or worm designed to activate under certain conditions.

5. A/An _____ is a virus designed to attach itself to the OS in and exhaust computer resources, especially CPU cycles.

6. _____ is a type of malicious software that gathers and reports information about a computer user discreetly and without the user's knowledge or consent.

7. _____ is the practice of conning people into revealing sensitive data on a computer system or information that can be used on networks and systems.

8. Sending bulk messages to recipients who have not solicited them is known as _____.

9. A/An _____ is a place where information goes into and out of a computer.

10. How would you differentiate a Trojan horse, a worm, and a virus?

    _____

    _____

    _____

    _____

11. What is social engineering?

    _____

    _____

    _____

    _____

12. What is a denial-of-service attack?

    _____

    _____

    _____

    _____

Hands-On Projects

1. Visit the Web site *www.insecure.org* to learn more about scanning.

2. Follow the rules to check for the authenticity of a Web site.

3. Scan your system with Adware, Spybot, and Malwarebytes (these are all reliable, free programs). Did they find any threats? Did they find the same threats?

Case Example

Ralph has been actively trading on the stock market this month. The stocks have been priced low and Ralph predicts a rally before the end of the quarter. He has been picking stocks aggressively and his stockbroker is trying hard to keep his funds in order.

When his broker calls him with information about a blue chip offload, Ralph decides to make the transaction at the coffee shop, which has wireless. He logs onto his bank account and does a third-party transfer to his broker, but first he checks to see if the site is secure and the browser has 128-bit encryption.

The next day, to his horror, he realizes that his account was reset and later the bank records show unauthorized third-party transfers.

1. What do you think went wrong with Ralph's account?

2. What are some of the possible ways that Ralph's account was compromised? Choose which of your answers is the most likely.

3. What would you advise Ralph if you were with him prior to the transaction?

Chapter 6

Incident Response

Objectives

After completing this chapter, you should be able to:

- Define an incident response
- Recall how to respond to different incidents

Key Terms

Boot sector virus   a program that replaces the boot program with a virus-infected version that loads and runs the virus in the memory of the computer

Incident   an incident is the occurrence of an event or set of events that threatens the security of a computer or computers

Incident response   the capability to deliver the event or set of events to an incident management system or a help desk system to solve the resulting problems, trace incidents, and plan and implement future prevention

Introduction

An *incident* is the occurrence of an event or set of events that threatens the security of a computer or computers. It can occur when one user tries to connect to another user for the purpose of data and resource sharing or when a hacker tries to gain undue advantage of resources on a computer over the Internet illegally. It also includes system crashes, which may have been caused by virus attacks, or unauthorized use of another user's account.

Floods, fires, electrical outages, and excessive heat are also incidents that can cause the systems to crash, but our concern in this chapter will be restricted to external security threats posed by hackers or intruders.

Whenever an incident is encountered, a certain set of procedures should be followed to

- keep track of the activities or events that occurred;
- complete an analysis of what happened, to determine the extent of the damage;

- determine how the incident happened; and

- determine what security measures should be taken in the future to prevent a similar incident.

This set of procedures is called the *incident response,* which, in summary, is the capability to deliver the event or set of events to an incident management system or a help desk system to solve the resulting problems, trace incidents, and plan and implement future prevention. In this chapter, we present several common incidents and then outline possible responses to them.

Incident: Trojan Attack

Ben uses his computer to send and receive e-mails and to save all his work-related documents. He receives an e-mail from his friend's e-mail address with an attachment named Openme.exe. After opening the attachment, pop-up windows that contain advertisements for adult Web sites start appearing frequently on his computer. Whenever he browses the Internet, he is prompted to download a phone dialer program. What could have happened?

It might be the W32.DSS.trojan program that was launched when he opened the attachment and that is now running on the system. The following section shows how to respond to this incident.

Response

1. End the Openme.exe process in the Task Manager by following these steps:

    a. Right click the taskbar and select **Task Manager.**

    b. Select the **Processes** tab.

    c. A list of processes will be displayed. Right click **Openme.exe,** and then click **End Process.**

    d. Click **Yes** when prompted for confirming the operation.

    e. Quit Task Manager.

2. Delete the Openme.exe file on your hard disk:

    a. Click **Start,** and then click **Search.**

    b. Click **All files and folders.**

    c. In the **All or part of the file name** box, type **Openme.exe.**

    d. In the **Look in** box, click the drive on which Windows is installed, and then click **Search.**

    e. Right-click the **Openme.exe** file that is listed, and then click **Delete.**

    f. Click **Yes** when prompted for confirming the deletion.

3. Remove the entry for Openme.exe in the Windows registry:

    a. Click **Start,** and then click **Run.**

    b. In the **Open** box, type **regedit,** and then click **OK.**

    c. Locate the following registry key:

    HKEY_LOCAL_MACHINE\SOFTWARE\Microsoft\Windows NT\CurrentVersion\Winlogon

4. Double-click **Shell entry** present in the right pane. The following values appear in the **Value data** box:

    Explorer.exe

    Openme.exe

5. Delete the **Openme.exe** value, and then click **OK.**

6. Quit Registry Editor.

1. Do not delete the **Explorer.exe** value.
2. The only value that should appear in the **Value data** box is **Explorer.exe.**

Incident: Boot Sector Virus Attack

After taking HTML classes in school, Jessica likes to create Web pages using her Windows XP system. She starts to create a Web page to showcase things about herself. While at school, she downloads some image files to put on her Web page from a net café and stores them on a floppy disk.

She brings the floppy home and puts it into her computer. She copies all the image files from the floppy to her system. When she tries to restart the system the next day, the system displays a blank screen. What could have happened?

The system is affected by a boot sector virus called FORMS. A *boot sector virus* is a program that replaces the boot program with a virus-infected version that loads and runs the virus in the memory of the computer.

The following is an outline of how to respond to this virus.

Response

Follow these steps to respond to a boot sector virus attack:

1. After shutting down Windows, remove the floppy disk from drive A.

2. Configure the order of the boot process to hard disk first, by entering the setup program.

3. To repair the boot sector, start the computer with an MS-DOS system disk and run the following command:

   fdisk /mbr

Incident: Home Page Settings Changed

Kim does a lot of research for her high school projects on her father's laptop. The laptop runs Windows XP, and Kim uses Internet Explorer to browse the Internet. One evening after she is done with her research, she closes the browser. But to her shock, when she tries opening the browser again the next day, a pornographic Web site opens. What could have happened?

It could have been:

- A virus that changed the home page (Figure 6-1).

- A malicious attack.

- Third-party software installed that changed the home page.

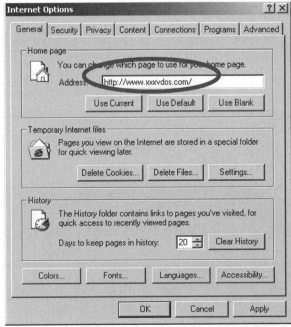

Source: www.microsoft.com

Figure 6-1 A home page that has been changed.

Following is how to respond to this incident of having a home page changed. If this change was caused by a virus, that will have to be dealt with as well.

Response

1. Open Registry Editor:

   a. Click **Start**, and then click **Run**.

   b. In the **Open** box, type **regedit**, and then click **OK**.

2. Locate the following registry key:

   HKEY_LOCAL_MACHINE\SOFTWARE\Microsoft\Internet Explorer\Main

3. Open the **Default_Page_URL** value (Figure 6-2).

4. Delete the value that is present (Figure 6-3).

5. Click **OK**.

6. Exit the registry.

7. Restart the system.

You can also view/change the home page of your browser from within it by going to **Tools, Internet Options**, as shown in Figure 6-4.

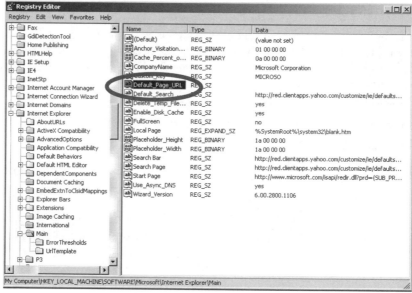

Source: www.microsoft.com

Figure 6-2   Registry Editor.

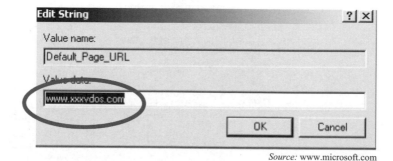

Source: www.microsoft.com

Figure 6-3   Editing Default_Page_URL.

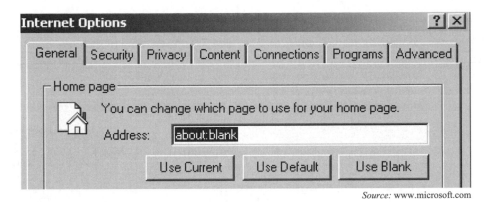

Source: www.microsoft.com

Figure 6-4   Changing the default home page within Internet Explorer.

Incident: Corrupted Registry

Allen's system runs Windows XP. He uses his system to browse the Internet and to check his e-mail. He usually gets a lot of forwarded mails from his friends. His friend forwards him an e-mail with the subject line, "This is too funny," and with an MPEG file attached. Allen immediately opens the attachment without scanning it. After finishing his work, he shuts down his system. The next day when he tries to start the system, the system will not boot and it displays the following error message:

Windows XP could not start because the following file is missing or corrupt: \WINDOWS\SYSTEM32\ CONFIG\SYSTEM

What could have happened? The attachment was probably a virus or Trojan that deleted system files or replaced them with corrupt versions. Here is a response to this error message.

Response

This response requires three different steps: backing up the registry, exporting the registry, and restoring the registry.

Backing up the Registry

1. The user must have either administrative privileges or be logged on as an Administrator.
2. Open System Restore:

   Start -> All Programs -> Accessories -> System Tools -> System Restore
3. Select **Create a restore point** from the two options listed (Figure 6-5).
4. Click **Next**.

Exporting the Registry

In Windows XP, the user can export the registry.

1. Open Registry Editor:

   a. Click **Start**, and then click **Run**.

   b. In the **Open** box, type **regedit**, and then click **OK**.
2. Select **Export** in the File menu.
3. The user can save this file into a registry file under the extension .reg.

Restoring the Registry

1. The user must have either administrative privileges or must be logged on as an Administrator.
2. Open System Restore:

   Start -> All Programs -> Accessories -> System Tools -> System Restore

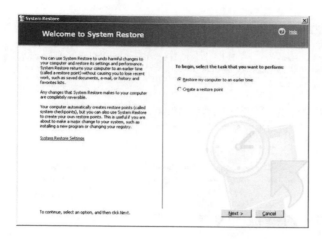

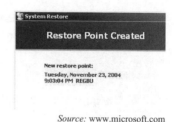

Source: www.microsoft.com

Figure 6-5   System Restore.

3. Select **Restore my computer to an earlier time** from the two options listed.

4. Click **Next**.

5. Select the restore point that has already been created.

Incident: CD Runs Automatically

Jason is in high school, and he spends most of his time and money on buying the latest games available on CDs. He has a computer with a built-in CD drive. One day, he gets a CD from one of his friends and plays it on his computer. The CD runs automatically, and to Jason's dismay, his system shuts down. The computer has a hard disk failure when he tries to reboot.

What might have happened? It is possible that the CD had an autorun.inf type virus that corrupted the drive. The following are steps to disable the autorun feature to avoid this consequence.

Response

There is no option available to enable or disable autorun in the user interface. The only way to disable autorun is by editing the registry. Figure 6-6.

1. Open Registry Editor:

   a. Click **Start**, and then click **Run**.

   b. In the **Open** box, type **regedit**, and then click **OK**.

Figure 6-6   Editing Autorun in Registry Editor.

2. Locate the following key:

   HKEY_LOCAL_MACHINE\System\CurrentControlSet\Services\Autorun

3. Change the **Autorun** value to 0. By default the value will be 1.

4. Restart the computer.

"Prevention Is the Best Medicine"

You should always remember that running, saving, or downloading a program from an unknown source can compromise the security of your system. The program might be any kind of malware. Be sure that your antivirus, spyware, and adware programs are up to date by downloading regular updates from the product Web sites.

If you connect to the Internet directly using a dial-up connection or any other connection, be sure to use a firewall. Firewalls do not detect malware that is present in the system already, but they do filter the Internet traffic that passes through the system. It is also a good security habit to regularly delete all Temporary Internet files, Cookies, and Internet History items.

In Windows XP with Internet Explorer version 7, choose the **Tools** menu, and then **Internet Options**. On the **General** tab there is a section called **Browsing History**. In that section there is a button called **Delete**. Click that and you will see another window that lists several items: **Temporary Internet Files**, **Cookies**, **History**, **Form data**, and **Passwords**. You can choose each one of these individually to remove the stored information, or you can choose the button at the bottom to **Delete All**, which does all of the above in one click.

With Internet Explorer version 6, from the **Tools** menu, **Internet Options**, the **General** tab has separate buttons to delete cookies, temporary files, and to clear the history.

Chapter Summary

- An incident is the occurrence of an event or set of events that threatens the security of a computer or computers.

- An incident can occur when one user tries to connect to another user for the purpose of data and resource sharing or when a hacker tries to gain undue advantage of resources over the Internet illegally.

- System crashes, virus attacks, and unauthorized use of another user's account are also examples of incidents.

- The incident response is a certain set of procedures that should be followed to

  - keep track of the activities or events that occurred;

  - complete an analysis of what happened, to determine the extent of the damage;

  - determine how the incident happened; and

  - determine what security measures should be taken in the future to prevent a similar incident.

- The user must always remember that running, saving, or downloading a program from an unknown source can compromise the security of a computer.

- Update antivirus, spyware, and adware programs regularly by going to the vendor's Web site.

- If the user is planning to connect to the Internet directly using a dial-up connection or any other connection, a firewall should be installed and turned on.

- It is also a good security habit to regularly delete all Temporary Internet files, Cookies, and Internet History items.

- There is no option available to enable or disable autorun in the user interface. The only way to disable autorun is by editing the registry.

Review Questions

1. What is an incident?

2. What are some common incidents that were discussed in the chapter? Can you name any others?

3. What is incident response?

4. How does the concept of vulnerability apply to the content of this chapter?

5. Why would you want to make a system restore point?

6. What are two locations where you can see what your browser home page is set to?

Hands-On Projects

1. Open the following key in the Windows registry and check the values:

   HKEY_LOCAL_MACHINE\SOFTWARE\Microsoft\Windows NT\CurrentVersion\Winlogon

2. Configure the order of the boot process with the hard disk first in the order.

3. Open the following key in the Windows registry and check the values:

   HKEY_LOCAL_MACHINE\SOFTWARE\Microsoft\Internet Explorer\Main

4. Which antivirus program is installed on your system? Update it with the latest definitions. Scan your computer after you have updated it.

5. Create a restore point in System Restore.

6. Open the following key in the Windows registry and check the values:

   HKEY_LOCAL_MACHINE\System\CurrentControlSet\Services\Autorun

7. Change the default autorun feature in Windows using Registry Editor.

Chapter 7

Secure Internet Access

Objectives

After completing this chapter, you should be able to:

- Restrict site access
- Identify a secure site
- Describe Internet content filtering software
- Enable Content Advisor
- Use ratings to define and limit content access
- Deal with cookies
- Use P2P networks securely
- Establish some security settings for a wireless network access point

Key Terms

Certificate authority   a trusted third party who issues digital certificates

Content Advisor   a tool in Internet Explorer that allows users to control the types of content that their computers can access on the Internet

Cookie   a piece of information sent by a Web server to a user's browser and stored on the user's hard disk; this information can be retrieved when the user returns to the Web site

Digital certificate   issued by the certificate authority, which confirms the identity of the dispatcher

Secure Socket Layer   a protocol developed by Netscape that enables a Web browser and a Web server to communicate securely

Service set identifier (SSID)   a sequence of characters that uniquely names a wireless local area network (WLAN)

Wired Equivalent Privacy   a security protocol for wireless local area networks that provides security by encrypting data over radio waves, so that it is protected as it is transmitted from one endpoint to another; WEP was designed to provide a similar level of security as that of a wired LAN

Case Example

David recently bought his son a personal computer for his birthday. He knows Alex is a smart kid and is excited about opening a world of information to him; however, he is also concerned about his son being exposed to Web sites that show or use offensive language, nudity, or sexual or violent content. Having heard about sex offenders lurking in cyberspace, he is concerned about Alex's safety.

Alex also shares a lot of music files over peer-to-peer networks like Kazaa. David would like to ensure that no hacker exploits this and uses the machine for unlawful purposes. Can David do something proactively to protect his son and the system from malicious use?

Can he set his software applications in such a way that they offer some extent of protection from security threats and attacks?

Introduction

Browsers need to be configured to ensure security because browsers can be used as a means of attack. Browsers can be used by attackers to automatically cause the recipient's computer to display the attacker's content, such as automatically opening (pop-up) advertising, displaying a pornography Web page, or resetting the default home page.

Attackers can also attempt a denial-of-service attack on the recipient's computer through HTML code that freezes or crashes the browser (or the entire computer). Attackers can use scripts to spoof Web pages and redirect the user to phishing sites, and malicious code, such as worms, can exploit flaws in the browser itself to cause harm to the system.

When Internet Explorer is installed, it considers all Web sites to be in a single zone—the Internet zone—and stands guard with a medium level of security. Sites can be classified into three other categories: local intranet, trusted sites and restricted sites. In this chapter, we will look at some of the security setting options in Internet Explorer to address various issues such as site filtering, content filtering, and guarding privacy on the Internet.

Basic Browser Security Settings

To increase security while browsing on the Internet with Internet Explorer, you can:

- Add a Web site to the list of trusted or restricted sites.
- Remove a Web site from a security zone.
- Change the security level of a zone.

Restricting Site Access

The restricted zone imposes the highest security level for sites the user deems untrustworthy. When these sites are visited, Internet Explorer will prompt the user at every turn.

Following are the steps to add a site to a particular zone—internet, local intranet, trusted sites, or restricted sites (Figure 7-1):

1. Go to the Web site you need to classify under a zone.
2. Copy the URL or the site address. Alternatively, you can type in the address directly if you know it.
3. On the Internet Explorer Tools menu, click **Internet Options**.
4. Click the Security tab, and then click the security zone to which the site is to be added:
   - Local intranet, trusted sites, or restricted sites. As all sites are by default already in the Internet zone, Web sites cannot be added to it.
5. Click the **Sites** button.
6. In the **Add this Web site to the zone** box, paste or enter the URL or site address in the box.
7. Click the **Add** button.

To view the list of Web sites added to trusted and restricted sites, click **Internet Options** on the Internet Explorer Tools menu. Click the **Security** tab, and then click either **Trusted sites** or **Restricted sites**. Click the **Sites** button to view the list.

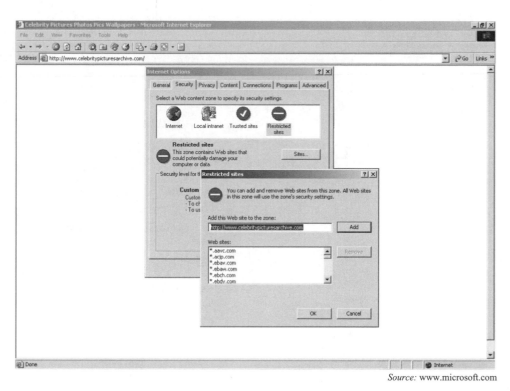

Source: www.microsoft.com

Figure 7-1　Restricting site access.

Removing a Site from a Security Zone

You can also choose to remove a Web site from a particular Web security zone. For example, if you mistakenly entered an external site as part of the internal network or assigned a trusted site status to an insecure site, you can remove it by following these steps (Figure 7-2):

1. On the Internet Explorer Tools menu, click **Internet Options**.
2. Click the Security tab, and then click the security zone from where the site needs to be removed: **Local intranet**, **Trusted sites**, or **Restricted sites**.
3. Click the **Sites** button.
4. In the **Web sites** box, click the name of the Web site to be removed.
5. Click the **Remove** button, and then click **OK** twice.

Changing the Security Level of a Zone

Internet Explorer can be set to different security levels and the levels can be customized. To accomplish this task, follow these steps (Figure 7-3):

1. On the Internet Explorer Tools menu, click **Internet Options**.
2. Click the **Security** tab, and then click the zone for which you want to change the security level.
3. Drag the slider to set the security level to high, medium, medium-low, or low; or click on the custom button to customize the settings for different options.

Internet Explorer describes each option to help you decide which level to choose and asks for confirmation when you change the restrictions.

Source: www.microsoft.com

Figure 7-2   Removing a site from a security zone.

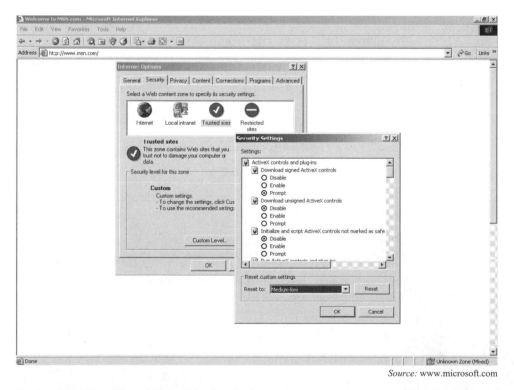

Source: www.microsoft.com

Figure 7-3   Changing the security level of a zone.

Identifying a Secure Web Site

In a brick-and-mortar store, you see the physical structure, the products, and the employees. You know who to go to if something should go wrong with your purchase; however, on the Internet, Web site visitors usually have no way of knowing much about the owner of the Web site. In an online purchase, customers want to know whom they will be paying. They want to authenticate the identity of the Web site owner and ensure that the personal information they send to the Web site cannot be intercepted by other Internet users.

Secure Socket Layer (SSL) is a protocol developed by Netscape that enables a Web browser and a Web server to communicate securely. It allows the Web browser to authenticate the Web server. In order for an SSL connection to be made, the SSL protocol requires the Web server to have a digital certificate installed on it.

This protocol assures a customer of three things:

1. *Authentication*: The Web site really is owned by the company that installed the certificate.

2. *Message privacy*: Using a unique "session key," SSL encrypts all information exchanged between the Web server and the customers, such as credit card numbers and other personal data. This key ensures that personal information cannot be viewed if it is intercepted by unauthorized parties.

3. *Message integrity*: The data cannot be tampered with by attackers over the Internet.

If a secure SSL connection is established between the Web browser and the Web server, the "http" in the Web address will usually change to "https" (Figure 7-4). When information is submitted to a secure Web site that does not have a valid SSL certificate, the browser will display a warning message.

If, however, a Web site is using a valid *digital certificate*, then the Web user will be informed that the Web site they are visiting has a digital certificate issued by a recognized *Certificate authority*—which is a trusted third party who issues the digital certificates—and that any data they submit to that site will be encrypted. By checking the certificate, the customer can verify that the Web site is valid and who it belongs to.

An SSL digital certificate contains the following information:

- The domain for which the certificate was issued
- The owner of the certificate (who is also the person/entity who has the right to use the domain)
- The physical location of the owner
- The validity dates of the certificate

If a site is secure, the browser will display a padlock icon near the bottom on the right side to indicate a secure site. The user does not have to install anything in particular or activate any service to use SSL. The SSL setting in Web browsers is turned on by default when the user visits a secure Web site. However, the user can upgrade the browser to a higher encryption standard, which you might do if you were managing many domains or need

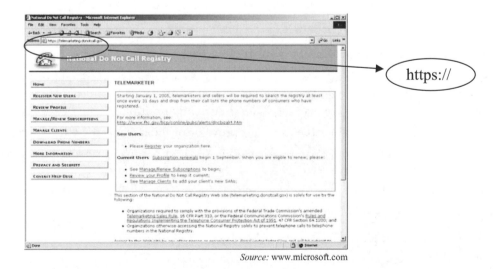

Source: www.microsoft.com

Figure 7-4   A Web page with the https designation.

to provide your customers with a higher level of assurance. There are many reasons and several types you can purchase depending on your specific needs.

Internet Filtering Software

Several tools are available that parents or guardians can employ to guide their children to safe and rewarding online experiences. Following are some of the terms you may come across while selecting software in this category:

- *Time Limiting*: limits time online
- *Filtering and Blocking*: limits access to some sites and words and images. Categories include:
  - *Sexually Explicit*—graphic descriptions or images of sexual nature
  - *Hate Groups*—groups advocating bigotry or hatred
  - *Graphic Violence*—violent images, language, bomb-building, etc.
  - *Criminal Activity*—promoting illegal activity
  - *Other Categories*—alcohol, games, advertising, politics, sports, etc.
- *Block Outgoing Content*: prevents kids from revealing personal information online
- *Browsers for Kids*: do not display inappropriate words or images
- *Kid-Oriented Search Engines*: perform limited searches or screen search results
- *Monitoring Tools*: alert adults to online activity without blocking access

One example is CyberPatrol parental control software, which is specifically designed to work on standalone Microsoft Windows–based PCs at either the desktop or laptop level. It allows you to manage and control children's access to the Internet as well as limit or prevent their access to programs, such as games or home finance packages located on your PC.

Configuring Internet Content Access

With Internet Explorer, you can configure your computer to limit access to specific types of content by using Content Advisor, a tool built into Internet Explorer, and by applying content rating levels.

Content Advisor

Content Advisor is a tool in Internet Explorer that allows users to control the types of content that their computers can access on the Internet. After Content Advisor is turned on, only rated content that meets or exceeds the user's criteria can be viewed. The settings can be adjusted to individual preferences.

The following shows how to access Content Advisor:

1. In Internet Explorer click Tools and then **Internet Options**.
2. Within **Internet Options** click the Content tab.

Within the **Content Advisor** window there are four tabs that can be used.

1. *Ratings*: This section allows a user to set the rating levels for language, nudity, sex, and violence. As you move the bottom slider from left to right, Internet Explorer will give you a brief description of what will be prohibited at the rating where the slider is currently positioned.
2. *Approved Sites*: This enables the user to approve or prohibit a specific URL from being viewed.
3. *General*: This allows the user to perform additional tasks such as setting up a supervisor password and implementing other system settings.
4. *Advanced*: This allows a user to obtain ratings from a ratings bureau and/or specify rules.

The following shows how to enable Content Advisor (Figure 7-5):

1. On the Internet Explorer Tools menu, click **Internet Options**.
2. Click the **Content** tab, and click the **Enable** button.
3. In the **Content Advisor** box, click the **General** tab, and then click the **Create Password** button.

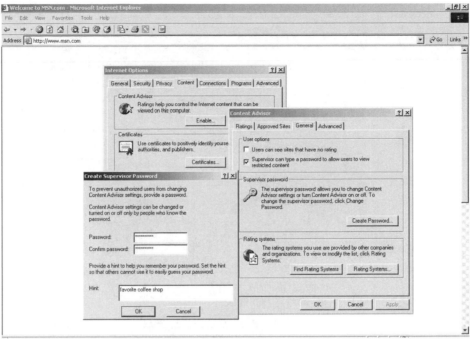

Figure 7-5   Enabling Content Advisor in Internet Explorer.

4. In the **Create Supervisor Password** box, type the password you want to use.

5. In the **Confirm password** box, type the same password again.

6. In the **Hint** box, type a hint to help you to remember your password, and then click **OK**.

7. Click **OK** in response to the message about Content Advisor, and then click **OK** once more.

Every time IE tries to access a restricted content site, the user will be prompted to type the supervisor password to get through.

Customizing Content Access Using Ratings

Ratings systems are available that can be added to the Content Advisor feature of Internet Explorer. To select content rating levels, follow these steps:

1. On the Tools menu, click **Internet Options**, and then click the **Content** tab.

2. In the **Content Advisor** area, click **Settings**.

3. In the **Password** box, type your supervisor password, and then click **OK**.

4. On the **Ratings** tab, select a category (**Language, Nudity, Sex,** or **Violence**) (Figure 7-6).

5. Drag the slider to the appropriate content level for the selected category.

6. The default setting for each category is Level 0, which is the most restrictive setting. Repeat steps 4 and 5 for each category.

Table 7-1 summarizes the ratings system in Content Advisor.

Understanding Cookies

A *cookie* is a piece of information sent by a Web server to a user's browser and stored on the user's hard disk. Cookies are a Web site's way of storing information on a user's machine for later retrieval. The pieces of information are stored as "name-value" pairs. A name-value pair is simply a named piece of data. It is not an executable program.

It is common for Web sites to generate a unique identification (ID) number for each visitor and store the ID number on each user's machine using a text file. This is an Internet cookie. In Windows XP, the cookies folder is in directory c:\windows\cookies (Figure 7-7).

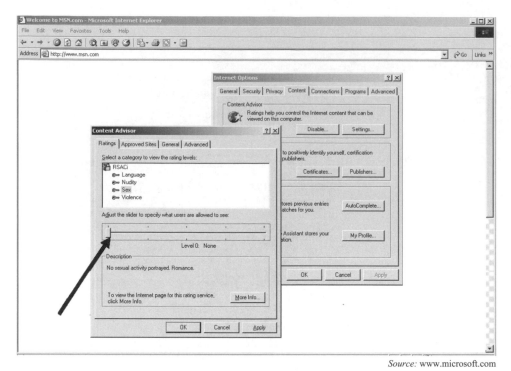

Source: www.microsoft.com

Figure 7-6 Setting the language, nudity, sex, or violence ratings in Content Advisor.

Level	Language Rating	Nudity Rating	Sex Rating	Violence Rating
4	Explicit or crude language	Provocative frontal nudity	Explicit sexual activity	Wanton and gratuitous violence
3	Obscene gestures	Frontal nudity	Nonexplicit sexual touching	Killing with blood and gore
2	Moderate expletives	Partial nudity	Clothed sexual touching	Killing
1	Mild expletives	Revealing attire	Passionate kissing	Fighting
0	Inoffensive slang	No nudity	No sexual acts	No violence

Table 7-1 Ratings System in Content Advisor

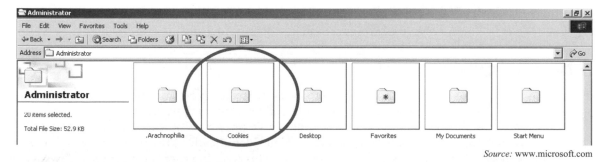

Source: www.microsoft.com

Figure 7-7 The Cookies folder in Windows.

Source: www.microsoft.com

Figure 7-8 Cookie settings.

Most sites store just one piece of information—a user ID—on the visitor's machine. But a site can store many name-value pairs if it wants to. For example, an online store may choose to store session information, session time information, and a cookie for each different page visited.

A Web site can retrieve only the information that it has placed on the machine. It cannot retrieve information from other cookie files, or glean any other information from the user's machine.

The following shows how a cookie works:

1. When the URL of a Web site is entered into the browser, the browser sends a request to the Web site for the page.

2. When the browser makes this request, it will search for a cookie file that Web site has set. If it finds a cookie file, the browser will send all of the name-value pairs in the file to the Web site's server along with the URL. If it finds no cookie file, it will send no cookie data.

3. The Web server receives the cookie data and the request for a page. If name-value pairs are received, the Web site can use them. If no name-value pairs are received, the Web site considers the user to be a new user. The server creates a new ID for the user in the Web site's database and then sends name-value pairs to the user's computer along with the Web page it sends. The name-value pairs are stored on the user's hard disk.

4. The Web server can change name-value pairs or add new pairs whenever the user visits the site and requests a page. There are other pieces of information, such as expiration date, path, etc., that the Web site can use as name-value pairs.

5. Users have control over this process. They can set an option in the browser so that the browser informs the user every time a site sends name-value pairs. The user can then accept or deny the values.

Cookie Settings

You can choose to set cookie preferences by going to **Internet Options** on the Tools menu of Internet Explorer (Figure 7-8). Click on the **Privacy** tab and set the slider to choose your preference. The **Settings** slider has six settings:

1. *Block All Cookies*: Cookies from all Web sites will be blocked, and existing cookies on the computer cannot be read by the Web sites that created them.

2. *High*: This setting blocks cookies that do not have a compact privacy policy or that have a compact privacy policy that specifies that personally identifiable information is used without the user's explicit consent.

3. *Medium High*: This setting blocks third-party cookies that do not have a compact privacy policy or that use personally identifiable information without the user's explicit consent. It blocks first-party cookies that have a compact privacy policy that specifies that personally identifiable information is used without explicit consent.

4. *Medium (default level)*: This setting blocks third-party cookies that do not have a compact privacy policy or that have a compact privacy policy that specifies that personally identifiable information is used without the user's explicit consent.

5. *Low*: First-party cookies that do not have a compact privacy policy are leashed (restricted so that they can only be read in the first-party context).

6. *Accept All Cookies*: All cookies will be saved on the computer, and existing cookies on the computer can be read by the Web sites that created them.

Information stored in a cookie is limited to whatever the user volunteers, such as filling out a form on a Web page to request information or buying something online. It is only a text file and cannot search a drive for information or carry a virus.

Deleting Cookies

You can also delete cookies by following these steps (Figure 7-9):

1. Start Internet Explorer.

2. On the Tools menu, click **Internet Options,** and then click the **General** tab.

3. In the **Temporary Internet files** section, click **Delete Cookies**, click **OK** twice.

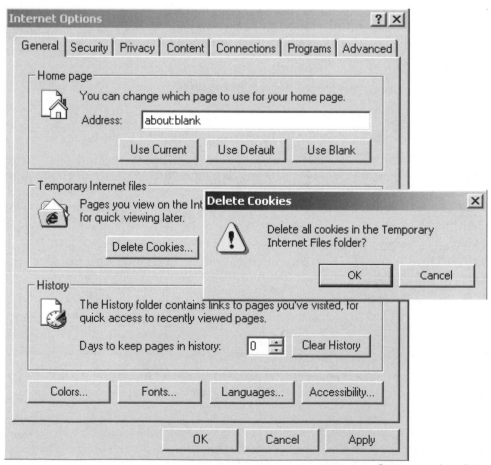

Source: www.microsoft.com

Figure 7-9   Deleting cookies.

Using P2P Networks Securely

If you are using a peer-to-peer (P2P) network to share files over the Internet, a few basic steps can help protect your system's security.

Use Reliable Client Software

Client software is often under continuous development and may have flaws that open the system to attacks. Installing the software might cause system crashes or other problems. It is possible that the client software is hosted from the participating user's machine and could be replaced with a malicious version that may install a virus or Trojan on the victim's computer; therefore, rely on software downloaded from reputable vendor sites.

Share Cautiously

When using P2P networks, there is generally a default folder for sharing designated during the installation. The designated folder should contain only files that are safe to be viewed on the P2P network. Many users unknowingly designate the root "C:" drive as their shared files folder, which allows everyone on the P2P network to see and access virtually every file and folder on the entire hard drive.

Scan Everything

All downloaded files must be treated with the utmost suspicion. There is no way of ensuring that the downloaded file is what it says it is or that it doesn't also contain some sort of Trojan or virus. It is important that a virus scan be performed using updated antivirus software on any file downloaded before it is executed or opened. It may still be possible that it could contain malicious code that the antivirus vendor is unaware of or does not detect, but scanning it before opening it will help prevent most attacks.

Choosing Appropriate Browser Settings

You should also be sure your browser settings are appropriate for the type of browsing you do. Follow these guidelines:

- Implement content settings in such a way that they do not affect your regular browsing. For example, if the Language setting is too restrictive, Web sites that deal with medical matters might be blocked. The objective with browser settings is to reach a balance between security and functionality.

- Restricting the placement of cookies on the computer might have an adverse effect on Web browsing. For example, if cookies are blocked, then the user will probably be unable to order items online. Cookies are meant to improve the Web surfing experience of users. Often it may be required to retrieve previous information—for example, if you have added items to the shopping cart and need to shop later.

- Choose the Autocomplete option only for Web addresses and *not for username and password forms*. It is not recommended to store passwords in your browser or use software that can help you fill in forms online in an automated manner. If there is a bug, or virus, that can compromise the access to these software applications, it is possible for your credentials to be stolen and misused.

Wireless Network Security Features

A wireless network is established by installing a wireless network access point, and wireless network adapters in the desktop or laptop computers. The access point is connected to your Internet service provider. The computers' wireless adapters locate it and use it to gain access to the Internet and other devices on your network. It works much the same as a wired network, but there are no cables (Figure 7-10).

Wired Equivalent Privacy (WEP) is a security protocol for wireless local area networks that provides security by encrypting data over radio waves, so that it is protected as it is transmitted from one endpoint to another (Figure 7-11). Wired Equivalent Privacy (WEP) is specified in the IEEE Wireless Fidelity (Wi-Fi) standard, 802.11b, and is designed to provide a wireless local area network (WLAN) with a level of security and privacy comparable to what is usually expected of a wired LAN.

Wireless network

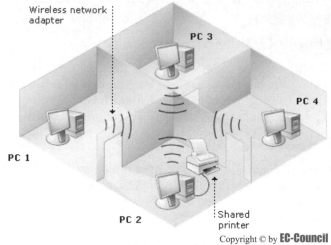

Figure 7-10 An example of a wireless network.

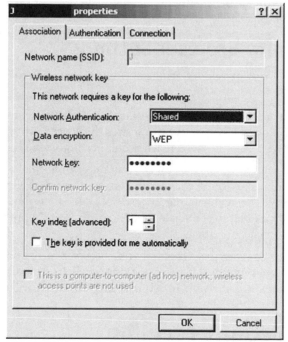

Source: www.microsoft.com

Figure 7-11 WEP settings.

Security Tip: Enable WEP. When setting up your wireless access point, you have a choice whether to enable WEP, and which authentication model to use. Open or shared keys can be used.

A *service set identifier (SSID)* is the name of a wireless local area network (WLAN). SSID is a sequence of characters that uniquely names a wireless local area network (WLAN). This name allows stations to connect to the desired network when multiple independent networks operate in the same physical area. All wireless devices on a WLAN must employ the same SSID in order to communicate with each other.

Security Tip: Use SSID. Change the default SSID name to uniquely identify your network.

Chapter Summary

- You can configure your browser settings to control site and content access in such a way that only content that you approve may be accessed.
- You can also control your privacy by restricting the placement of cookies by Web sites.
- You can choose to adopt a ratings system to ensure that undesirable content is not served by the browser.
- A secure site uses SSL and can be identified by the https:// designation in the URL. You must always look for https:// in the URL and the padlock sign on your browser when you surf secure sites where confidential information may be shared.
- Ensure that only minimal information is revealed to a Web site to limit cookie content. You can control your privacy further by being cautious of the information you share with a Web site.
- Limit sharing and scan all content on a P2P network. This precaution is essential to avoid being compromised by malicious content.
- Use WEP and SSID if connected to a wireless network.

Review Questions

1. In Internet Explorer, Web sites can be categorized into what four zones?

   _____

   _____

   _____

   _____

2. The _____ zone imposes the highest security level.

3. _____ is a protocol developed by Netscape that enables a Web browser and a Web server to communicate securely.

4. What are two signs that indicate a site is secure?

   _____

   _____

   _____

   _____

5. _____ software can be used to protect children while they browse the Internet.

6. SSL assures an online customer of what three things?

   _____

   _____

   _____

   _____

7. _____ is a tool in Internet Explorer that allows users to control the types of content their computers can access.

8. Content ratings are available for what four types of content?

   _____

   _____

   _____

   _____

9. What is a cookie?

   _____

   _____

   _____

   _____

10. Where are cookies commonly stored on a computer?

    _____

    _____

    _____

    _____

11. What are the six privacy settings for cookies?

    _____

    _____

    _____

    _____

12. What three steps should you take to protect your computer's security when you are sharing files on a P2P network?

    _____

    _____

    _____

    _____

13. What does SSID stand for?

    _____

    _____

    _____

14. What does WEP do?

_____

_____

_____

_____

15. In which IEEE Wireless Fidelity (Wi-Fi) standard is WEP specified?

_____

_____

_____

_____

Hands-On Projects

1. Restrict a particular Web site using Internet Explorer.

2. Activate the Content Advisor.

3. Remove a Web site from a particular zone using Internet Explorer.

4. Configure Noah's Web-Kid Web Browser.

5. Enable WEP in a wireless network.

6. Set the privacy settings for cookies such that it blocks first-party cookies that use personally identifiable information without explicit consent.

7. Delete the cookies in the Temporary Internet Files folder.

8. Visit _https://www.paypal.com/_ and note the features of a secure site.

Chapter 8

Working on the Internet

Objectives

After completing this chapter, you should be able to:

- Use various options and devices while working on the Internet
- Work safely in Web-based and mail client e-mail systems
- Send or transfer information and files safely
- Transact business safely
- Communicate safely
- Use portable, wireless, and USB devices; media files; and third-party software safely

Key Terms

Asymmetric encryption   the key used to encrypt a message differs from the key used to decrypt it, a public key and a private key. The private key is kept secret, while the public key may be widely distributed. Messages encrypted with the public key can only be decrypted with the corresponding private key. The keys are related mathematically, but the private key cannot be derived from the public key.

Cipher   an algorithm for data encryption and decryption

Cryptographic algorithm   a set of guidelines used to execute cryptographic operations such as encryption and decryption

Digital signature   code, attached to an encrypted message, that is used to validate the identity of the dispatcher

Instant messenger   a computer application that allows instant text communication between two or more people through a network

Key   a character or sequence of characters applied to text in order to encrypt or decrypt it

Private key   the private key is used to digitally sign data, or to decrypt data that has been encrypted with the corresponding public key

Public key   widely distributed key used to encrypt messages that can only be decrypted with the corresponding private key and through this process confirms the digital signature

Symmetric encryption   an encryption algorithm that uses the same secret key for both encryption and decryption; the sender and receiver must share a key in advance

Web Distributed Authoring and Versioning (WebDAV)   an open Internet protocol that allows clients on a PC or Mac to access files and folders on a server, as on a desktop, while they actually reside on a remote server accessed via the Web

Web folders   WebDAV client that allows files and folders to be available on a Web server using Windows authentication for greater access

Case Example

Denise considers herself to be computer savvy and uses her computer extensively for several activities. She pays many of her bills online. She has registered with her bank for third-party payments and believes that this practice reduces the risk of using her credit card online. The bank directly debits her account and pays the third party.

This morning when she checks her e-mail, she has an e-mail alert from her telephone company to pay her telephone bill promptly and receive a 10% discount on her bill. Denise clicks the link that takes her to the familiar e-payment site.

She keys in her authentication credentials and is surprised when told that her details do not match the record. She goes back to her e-mail to check if she has followed the correct steps, when she notices another e-mail asking her to patch her system to ensure a secure transaction. Denise installs the patch and when she enters the e-payments Web site address manually again, it lets her log in!

She opts for a direct debit; it takes her to the familiar merchant login page where she keys in her bank customer identification and password to make the payment. She prints her receipt and files it.

What do you suppose the patch added that made it possible for Denise to log in? Do you think she has a secure connection? How would she be able to tell if it was safe for her to type her bank id and password in the Web page form?

Introduction

In this chapter, we discuss how to work safely on the Internet, including sending or transferring information and files; transacting business; communicating via instant messaging or file-sharing and dial-in networks; using portable, wireless, and USB devices; and using media files and third-party software.

Principles of Security

Secure information will have the following characteristics:

- *Confidentiality*: only those authorized have access to the information
- *Integrity*: information is not tampered with or changed in an undesirable manner
- *Availability*: information is available to legitimate users
- *Nonrepudiation*: ensures the origin or ownership of the information
- *Authenticity*: ensures the authenticity of the information

For example, if your bank sends you an account statement, you can say it was received securely if:

- Only you have access to it. The bank sent the statement to you using a digitally signed message and delivered it to an inbox to which you have the sole access. You can say that the message is confidential.
- The bank statement is unchanged in form and content from the time it was dispatched until it reached your inbox. You can say that the integrity of the message is intact because the original content has not been altered by the time you receive it.
- The bank sent the statement to you and you—only you—were able to access it because the security of it defined that you are the only legitimate user. You can say that the message has been made available to you—the intended recipient.

- The bank is able to confirm that it was the entity that sent the message to you. In other words, the originator of the message acknowledges the origin of the message, which is called nonrepudiation.

- You know that the information you received is true and authentic.

Encryption

Encryption is the process of transforming data into an unrecognizable form by using an algorithm called a cipher and a variable value called the key. The *key* is a character or sequence of characters applied to text in order to encrypt or decrypt it. Decryption is reversing the encryption process to restore the original data form. A *cipher* is an algorithm for performing encryption (and the reverse, decryption). It is a series of well-defined steps that can be followed as a procedure. The variable key is used to change the details of the algorithm process.

A key is a piece of information that controls the operation of a *cryptographic algorithm,* or a set of guidelines used to execute cryptographic operations such as encryption and decryption. A minimum key length of 80 bits is necessary for strong security with symmetric encryption algorithms. 128-bit keys are considered very strong and recommended for being more secure.

Symmetric encryption uses the same cryptographic key to encrypt and decrypt the message, so the sender and receiver must share a key in advance. The advantage of symmetric encryption is that it is faster; however, the downside is that it is shared between two people and is susceptible to compromise. In *asymmetric encryption,* a *private key* and a *public key* are used. The user issues a public key widely for distribution. Anyone can use it to encrypt messages to be sent to the user and to confirm the user's digital signature. The private key is used to digitally sign data or to decrypt data that has been encrypted with the corresponding public key. The sender alone knows the private key while the public key is known to all (Figure 8-1).

Digital Certificates

When Alice wants to send Bob an encrypted message, she writes the message and encrypts it by signing it with her private key. Bob does not know the private key, so he needs a related key or the same key to decrypt the message. Alice's private key has a related pair—called the public key. The public key can be registered with a third-party agency, called a certification authority, so that people like Bob can verify that it is indeed Alice's public key. He can then use the public key to decrypt the message and read it. If Alice sent the message to Bob and Ray, Ray can also use the public key to read the message.

A digital certificate is the electronic identification of an individual or entity (Figure 8-2). In the previous example, the certification authority that Alice registers with to validate her key issues a digital certificate that verifies her identity. It contains information such as the following:

- Sender's public key
- Sender's name
- Expiration date of sender's public key
- Name of certificate-issuing body
- Serial number of certificate
- Digital signature of the issuer

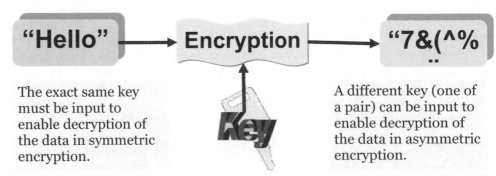

Figure 8-1   Encryption uses a variable value called a key.

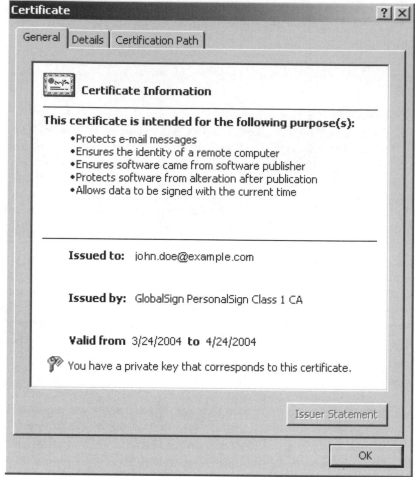

Source: www.microsoft.com

Figure 8-2   A digital certificate.

The function of the certification authority is to guarantee that when a user downloads a file or opens a message sent from a sender, the sender is genuine and not someone who has forged his signature. The certification authority verifies the identity and sends the digital certificate, which contains information about the sender's identity and a copy of the sender's public key. The certificate in turn is encrypted by the certification authority's private key.

Digital Signatures

A *digital signature* is a cryptographic means of authentication; it is code, attached to an encrypted message, that is used to validate the identity of the dispatcher. When a person signs a document with a digital signature, a software program will append that person's digital signature and digital certificate to the document. The recipient can check the authenticity with a certification authority. When a recipient receives the file containing the sender's digital signature and certificate, he can verify that no one has forged the document. Software is used to verify the digital signature by comparing the sender's public key, contained in their digital signature, with the copy contained in the sender's digital certificate.

The following shows how to create a free digital signature (Figure 8-3):

1. Visit *http://www.pgp.com/downloads/freeware/* to download PGP (Pretty Good Privacy) freeware to generate a key.

2. Upload the signed private key to a public key ring so that others can verify the digital signature.

3. Digitally sign outgoing e-mail messages. You can import the key to the e-mail client.

```
-----BEGIN PGP PUBLIC KEY BLOCK-----
Version: 2.7

mQCNAi3DID8AAAEEAM1cij7N6KgDsJnH8sANhk
A2dr6eMaL9Q1c3aTc8AGD37ZA78wvIyoOr5Oiz
AExfMgVlOZwmIGZsURsZ2nlvG/ksfylDdU3F3t
tCJSdXNzZWxsIE51bHNvbiA8bmVsc29uQGNyeU
NxjaDtyBAQGdwgP/RjPZ67+zwOZWd2OqGnOniz
WbOSuoMYsEYPT4G4igdoPCVjGbwd3WWPN22C/Q
/bFSIpW8TO2ClGTppUx3iaI6tIYd/armWhFPB2
BRAt4CArpsFJZIOUJOEBAQeQA/9yl+SvMn7bVI
SiAhfXukETra3f2rv71uNopfluB9MOOWOBSq3B
r7WbQNwqjBJtaNBTzfQIijK3MXYfIcFTkpDNKk
KWXgtw==
=xE3S
-----END PGP PUBLIC KEY BLOCK-----
```

Figure 8-3 A digital signature.

E-Mail

When using e-mail you need to keep the basics of security that we have been discussing in mind: authentication, privacy, and integrity. This section will explain how to work safely in Web-based and mail client e-mail systems.

Web-Based E-Mail

Most of us are familiar with Web-based e-mail—Hotmail, Yahoo mail, Gmail, etc. How do you ensure that your access is secure and that your e-mail is not intercepted or read by others when you use Web-based e-mail? Use these precautions:

1. Check if your Web mail provider offers you a secure login option. If so, use the secure method to login. If you are on a network, it is possible for an intruder to "sniff" the network and intercept your credentials if they are sent in clear text and not encrypted.
2. Even while using Web mail, try to adopt an encryption method such as PGP to sign your documents so that even if the message is intercepted, it will not be easy to decipher.
3. Check if your Web mail provider offers third-party secure authentication methods such as SecureID.
4. Look for an SSL-enabled connection while accessing mail through secure channels. You can verify this type of connection by checking for https:// and the padlock sign.

Mail Client E-Mail

E-mail clients are popular among Internet users. It can come bundled along with a browser or installed separately. Many e-mail clients come with security and privacy options. In the case of Outlook (part of Microsoft Office), users have the option of enabling only secure content and also to enable encryption in e-mail. Though we know e-mail clients have been attacked repeatedly because this information has been published in vulnerability disclosures, efforts are being made to enable security by default. For instance, Outlook 2002 and 2003 are set to "Restricted Sites" by default with regard to secure content. This disables automatic scripts from running. You can enable secure content by opening **Outlook -> Tools -> Options -> Security -> Secure content.**

Enable encryption of contents and attachments using S/MIME and any digital certificate you possess. S/MIME is a protocol that can help you encrypt your message contents and is based on public key cryptography. You can access Outlook's S/MIME settings by opening **Outlook -> Tools -> Options -> Security -> Settings -> My S/MIME Settings (your e-mail).**

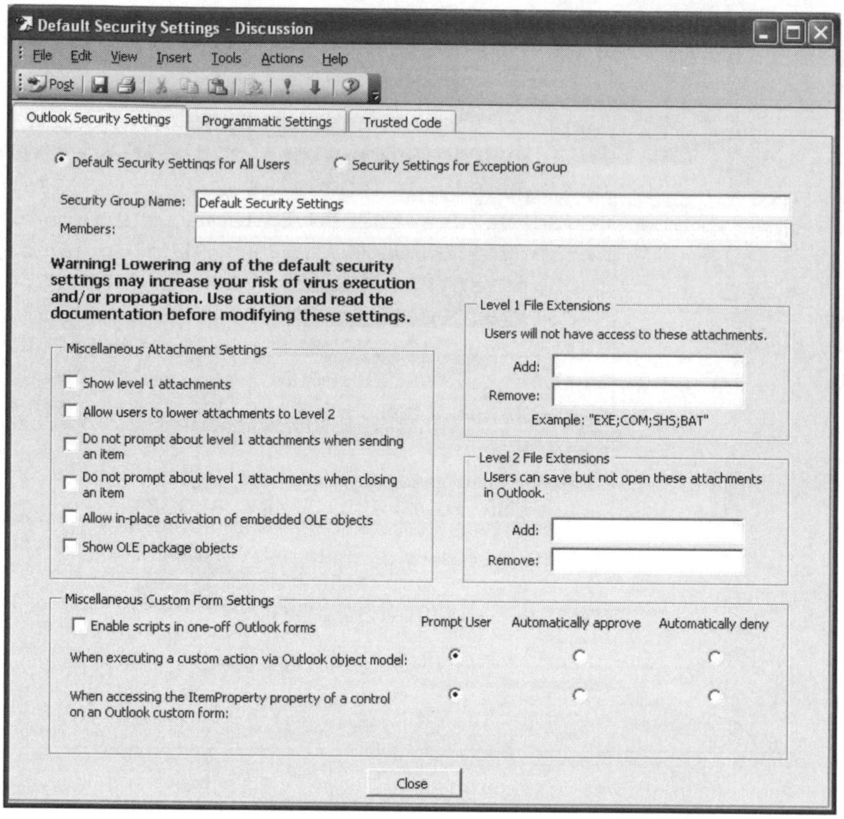

Source: www.microsoft.com

Figure 8-4   Outlook security settings.

Apart from this precaution, you can use Outlook security settings to configure attachment settings and automatic access to contact addresses by other programs (Figure 8-4).

File Transfer

If you need to transfer large files over the Internet, you have several options. This section looks at two of the options: FTP and Web folders.

File Transfer Protocol (FTP)

File Transfer Protocol (FTP) is one of the protocols belonging to the TCP/IP suite of protocols that is used to copy files between two computers, typically over the Internet; it is an easy way to transfer files to a storage site such as a Web server. FTP can be used for both uploading and downloading files. There are several FTP clients available that make it easier to execute the FTP commands.

Most browsers also allow users to browse FTP sites. However, the disadvantage with FTP is that it sends credentials in clear text, which can be intercepted and used by an intruder. In Internet Explorer the form used is ftp://username:password@hostname. Having the password in the URL field is a security risk and is not recommended.

FTP clients are available that allow secure access using Secure Shell protocol. If you are using FTP regularly, you should use a secure FTP client. You should also check if the Web site is using an FTP server that is secure and cannot be broken into. Preferably, it should not allow anonymous login because there is no way of knowing who accesses the resources. WinSCP is an open-source secure FTP client for Windows using SSH (Figure 8-5). Its main function is the safe copying of files between a local and a remote computer (*http://winscp.sourceforge .net/eng/index.php*).

Web Folders

Web folders are files and folders that are available on a Web server using Windows authentication for greater access security. They are supported in Windows 98/2000/NT/ME/XP and Mac OS X. *Web Distributed*